MAGIC WORDS IN HYPNOSIS

THE SOURCEBOOK OF HYPNOSIS PATTER AND SCRIPTS AND HOW TO OVERCOME HYPNOTIC DIFFICULTIES

RICHARD K. NONGARD
Bestselling Author of *Medical Meditation: How to Reduce Pain and Recover Faster from Illness*

Richard K. Nongard

Magic Words
The Sourcebook of Hypnosis Patter and Scripts and How to Overcome Hypnotic Difficulties

By Richard K. Nongard, LMFT, CCH

Foreword by Hugh Cole, Ph.D.

Text Copyright © 2011 by Richard K. Nongard

Edited by James Hazelrig (www.HarmonyHypnosis.net)

ISBN 978-1-257-80763-5

First Printing March 2011

Second Printing July 2011

Printed in the United States of America

by PeachTree Professional Education, Inc.

All rights reserved.

No part of this publication may be reproduced, stored in a retrieval system or transmitted in any form or by any means—electronic, mechanical, photocopy, recording or any other—without the prior written permission of the publisher. The only exception is brief quotations in printed reviews.

    PeachTree Professional Education, Inc.
        7107 S. Yale, Ste 370
        Tulsa, OK 74136
        (800) 390-9536
    www.SubliminalScience.com
    www.LearnClinicalHypnosis.com

All hypnotherapists are not created equal.

When you learn with Richard K. Nongard, you are learning with one of the top hypnotherapists in the country.

Richard K. Nongard is an innovative leader in the fields of psychotherapy and hypnosis. Since beginning his career in the late 1980s, he has trained literally thousands of professionals, including psychologists, medical doctors, ministers, social workers, family therapists, hypnotherapists and professional counselors in ways to do a better job serving their clients.

Nongard has authored many hypnosis and psychotherapy textbooks, videos and professional educational materials, and is the creator of the SuccessFit® Weight Loss Trance-Formation program, and the QuitSuccess® Tobacco Cessation Treatment Program, used by hospitals and healthcare groups across the country.

He holds advanced degrees in both counseling and religion, and has trained in the USA, Canada and Europe. He is a former Disciples of Christ minister, and has worked as a substance abuse counselor, a marriage and family therapist, and as a consultant to dozens of criminal justice departments. He is also the President of the International Certification Board of Clinical Hypnotherapy.

You may contact Richard at (800) 390-9536, or visit his website at www.SubliminalScience.com

Richard K. Nongard

About the ICBCH

The International Certification Board of Clinical Hypnotherapy is a worldwide organization with thousands of members that include professional hypnotists, psychotherapists, social workers and counselors. We offer hypnosis training and education through live hypnosis seminars, online classes and home study courses on subjects related to hypnosis, NLP (Neuro-linguistic Programming), medical meditation and professional life coaching. Each year the ICBCH holds an annual convention and also accredits schools and organizations that provide hypnosis training. You can become a certified hypnotherapist through the ICBCH by visiting:
  www.HypnotherapyBoard.org

Our Internet forum can be found at www.ICBCHForum.com

TABLE OF CONTENTS

Foreword   11

Introduction   13

STRUCTURE = PREPARATION FOR SUCCESS   19

PRETALK   21
Welcome   23
Complete Forms
Collect Payment
Find Out Experience with Hypnosis
How They Heard about You
Positive Reinforcement   24
Explain Hypnosis
Answer Questions
Convincers   26

ASSESSMENT   32
Intake / Interview
Specific Tools

INDUCTION   36
Eye Fixation or Eye Closure
Progressive Relaxation   38
Autogenic Experience   41
Creative Visualization Tailored to Learning Style   42
Learning Styles   43

DEEPENER   45
Number Count
Ratify Hypnosis   49
A Comment on the "Sleep" Command   53

SUGGESTIVE THERAPY 54
Indirect Suggestion
Transitional Deepening Suggestion 57
Ego-Strengthening 59
Direct Suggestion 60
Hypnotic Phenomena 65
Post-Hypnotic Suggestion 68

AWAKENING 71
Orientation to Surroundings
Energize
Direct Suggestion to Open Eyes

AFTER THE SESSION 73
Check for Time Distortion—Proof
Review Suggestions 75
Schedule Next Appointment 76

A NOTE ABOUT PRACTICE 77

KEY ELEMENTS FOR EFFECTIVE PATTER AND SCRIPT BUILDING 79
Positive Suggestions

Clear Concepts 81

Present Tense, Strengths and Resources 83

Realistic, Practical and Healthy 84

Engage All Senses 85

Individualized, Customized Suggestions 86

Utilize Dominant Emotions 88

SUGGESTIVE PATTER: PHRASES, CONCEPTS, AND ANSWERS   91

When Meeting a New Client who has Never been Hypnotized   92

When Meeting a New Client who has been Previously Hypnotized by Someone Else   93

When the Client is Anxious   94

When a Client has Doubts   95

Words that Normalize Hypnosis   96

Words that Define Hypnosis for Clients   97

To Help Clients Feel Safe   98

To Let Clients Know They are in Control   99

To Establish your Role   100

Words to Reverse Role   101

To Get Paid   102

When a Client is Not Prepared to Pay Today   103

When Questioned about High Fees   105

Do you have a Guarantee?   106

When There is Background Noise   107

How to Prepare for Potential Interruptions   108

What if a Cell Phone Rings During the Session   109

When Time is Short   110

When a Client is Sleepy   111

To Avoid Clients Falling Asleep   112

When a Client is Emotional   113

When a Client is Unfocused   114

When a Client's Mind is Wandering   115

When Client Say They are More Comfortable in an Odd Position   116

To Put Clients into Hypnotic Posture   117

What if a Client's Legs or Arms are Crossed   119

When Clients Do Not Close their Eyes   120

When Clients Do Not Follow Initial Suggestions in Preparation and Induction   121

When Clients Laugh During Induction   122

What if a Client Says, "I Just Can't Do This"   123

What if Clients Say They Aren't Hypnotized   125

To Help Clients Who Struggle with Letting Go   126

To Give Clients a Self-Directed Exit   127

When Clients Swallow, Scratch, Itch, or Fidget During a Session   128

If a Client "Twitches" or has a Muscle Spasm   129

When Clients Sneeze During the Session   130

To Deal with Tears During Trance   131

To Deal with Intense Unpleasant Emotion   133

To Change your Plan or Style to a New One   134

To Introduce a Written Script   135

To Set Up a Story, Parable, or Metaphor   136

To Read from a Script   137

To Transition to Direct Suggestion   138

To Deepen Trance   139

To Count to the Deepest Level of Trance   140

When Clients won't Go into Deep Trance   141

To Create Hypnotic Experience   142

To Create Comfort   143

To Help Clients Realize they are Going into Hypnosis   144

To Manifest Initial Hypnotic Phenomena   145

To Facilitate Two-Way Communication   146

To Keep Client Awake During Mid-Session   147

Magic Words

To Decrease Resistance at any Time in the Process   148

To Employ a Double Bind   149

To Validate Progress   150

To Give Client Ownership of Suggestions   151

To Compound Suggestions   152

To Avoid Sounding like a Psychic or a Fortune Cookie   153

To Have Client Take Action in Hypnosis   154

To Tap into Unconscious Resources   155

To Give Universal Reinforcers   156

How to Give a Post-Hypnotic Suggestion   158

How to Transition from Deep Trance to End of Session   159

To Make Sure the Client is Stable Following a Session   160

To Schedule the Next Visit   161

To Step out of the Room Mid-Session   162

FINAL THOUGHTS   163

APPENDIX A: SAMPLE INTAKE QUESTIONS   164

APPENDIX B: ADDITIONAL ASSESSMENT TOOLS   167

Richard K. Nongard

FOREWORD

Richard Nongard once again has produced a wonderful information-dense book that makes sense out of the world of "scriptnosis." Too often in hypnotherapy we think of scripts as a sort of a "magic patter" to be read word-for-word to our clients as they dream passively in our comfy recliners. And too often this leads to a limited understanding of our work as hypnotherapists, by providing cookie cutter solutions and cookie cutter attitudes toward clients with outwardly similar issues, for inwardly complex and different emotional needs.

Richard elucidates the true nature of hypnotic patter by providing the loose skeleton upon which a client's beliefs and emotions are hung. He breaks down our interactions with a client to show the role of "hypnotic patter," from the moment of first contact with a client to the all-important exit interview. Richard not only shows you how to write your own thoughtful and artfully directed scripts, but he also neatly packages the gems of a hypnotherapist's toolbox, i.e. those little answers to questions they didn't know they wanted to ask.

As a practicing hypnotherapist with a long track record of success, as well as a versatile instructor of all things hypnotic, Richard is keen to share with you the practical, real world of hypnotherapy. He is results-oriented, and he makes you think of all the ways you can become a better hypnotherapist. I recommend his work not only to beginning hypnotherapists, but also to the rest of us "seasoned professionals" who might want to take our practice to another level.

~ Hugh Cole, PhD

Hugh Cole, Ph.D., is a Harvard-trained life coach and health coach with a proven track record in helping clients lose weight and control diabetes. He has a Ph.D. from Rutgers University and spent his career working in biochemistry. He is uniquely qualified to assist people in reaching weight loss goals.

Magic Words

INTRODUCTION

I have been using hypnotherapy in one form or another with a wide variety of clients for the last twenty years, but before I ever studied hypnosis, I paid my way through college doing magic tricks at children's parties. In truth, the two professions share a certain similarity; in each, my job is to say the "magic words" needed to elicit the desired responses from my listeners.

Most brand new hypnotists learn to perform hypnosis by reading aloud from a script. A bit nervously, they intone the words written on the page before them, careful to read the "magic spell" verbatim. Upon running out of text, the hypnosis student looks up from the page to see whether or not the magic words have worked. Of course, this isn't the most effective way to do hypnosis, but it is how most of us learned.

In contrast to how hypnotists are trained using scripts, stage magicians are trained to use patter. When a budding magician buys a trick at the magic store, it comes with a "patter sheet." Instead of being a strict script to be read verbatim, it is a list of contingencies and how to handle them. The purpose of a patter sheet is not to merely walk magic students through an ideal performance, but to prepare them for all eventualities—by giving them the "magic words" needed for every situation.

The crucial difference between these two approaches is that magicians are taught from the beginning how to think on their feet and how to structure patter; hypnotists usually have to figure it out on their own.

I train a lot of hypnotherapists, and the newer ones are usually frustrated by what they perceive as an inability to really grasp how to structure suggestions. They just aren't sure exactly what to say or how to say it, and they wish they could conjure up the "magic words" for a session to make it more effective.

Well, *Voilà!* Here they are. This book is all about helping you to maximize the benefit to your clients in every hypnotherapy session. It's designed to teach you how to put together the best session possible, by choosing the right words or phrasing patter.

Please understand, this is not a traditional script book full of verbatim scripts from start to finish. This is a book of patter or script language samples, so you can learn to structure and adapt your own personal style or approach with content that will be useful for a variety of conditions.

If you are interested in complete verbatim induction and deepening scripts, I recommend my book called, *Inductions and Deepeners: Styles and Approaches for Effective Hypnosis*. And for those looking for a resource of complete suggestive therapy scripts, I recommend John Cerbone's book, *Hypnotic Scripts that Work*.

I personally write a lot of hypnosis scripts, as did Milton Erickson. It is interesting to see how hypnotherapists have somewhat rewritten the history or mystique concerning Erickson, who was one of the founders of medical hypnosis. In doing so, they have attributed many patterns of communication to him as if they were all spontaneously derived, based only on the clients' presentation during sessions.

In reality, Erickson wrote many scripts. His philosophy was that a good hypnotherapist should take all of his or her scripts, all of their writings, and pare them down each year to the most effective scripts and stories and metaphors that worked successfully in their hypnotherapy sessions—the magic words—and reuse them whenever appropriate with other clients later.

And so, following this philosophy, in this book I will share with you how I structure sessions, how I write scripts, and how I employ patter to handle any situation.

Before we begin with the details of structure and content, however, let me paint a picture for you of my clinical office. In addition to the comfy over-sized recliner and love seat for clients, I have a small side desk with space to write, but its function is primarily to hold my sound equipment. I always use headphones and a microphone with my clients to help them detach even further and really focus on the words I use. I have a candy dish full of cough drops for the smokers. I have them suck on a cough drop before each session, because otherwise they *will* cough, and it can be distracting. I have a bookshelf adorned with interesting books and knick-knacks, which can provide both ice-breaking conversation and focal points for trance induction.

I have all these things in my office because they are part of what helps me insure that I'm able to give the client everything they came for during the hypnosis session. These are my tools of the trade. And just like all these other items, scripts and outlines (abbreviated scripts) are important tools to aid in success with the client. I view an outline as a guide to help me make sure that in every one of my sessions I cover everything that is important to the client, and to make sure I don't miss anything.

I think sometimes it's a matter of pride for folks to say, "I never use scripts in hypnosis or hypnotherapy; I do everything off the top of my head and just by reading the client's needs." Well, that may appear very intelligent or like you're a hypnosis superstar, but personally, I want to make sure that my clients receive everything they came—and they came for me to make effective suggestions to them during the course of their hypnotherapy sessions—so I don't mind using a 'cheat sheet' script, and my clients don't mind either.

There are certain things in this book that I want to cover, and I'm not going to miss any of them because I have written them out in an outline. And you're glad that I have sketched out my plan because it will make certain that you receive everything that is important to you in purchasing this book, because I was prepared when I started writing it. It's the same principle.

Even with smoking and weight loss clients—and believe me I've done hundreds and hundreds of these sessions and even written scripts for other hypnotherapists to use with their clients on these subjects—I still bring my scripts with me. (We'll talk more about individual client assessment later, and you'll understand more about why I think scripting is so important even for the most common sessions.)

Now please don't misunderstand—I do not sit through each session with the microphone and read to them word for word verbatim from a twenty-page script, but I do have notes in my hand or on the desk next to me, and at various times during the process I may read specific things to them. During the pre-talk with clients I explain:

> *I'm going to bring some papers in with me that contain some suggestions I'm going to make to you, based on our conversations about your goals. These aren't suggestions that come from me, but rather they are things that you want me to suggest, based on the fact that you came here and scheduled this appointment, and I want to make sure that we don't miss anything during the session.*

Essentially, I took some notes and have some interesting related stories to share, and at various times during our session you may actually even hear me reading some of these things to you, and that's because I want to make certain that you receive all the help you need.

My clients really appreciate it when I bring a script or outline, as it shows that I am prepared for my therapy session with them.

Richard K. Nongard

STRUCTURE = PREPARATION FOR SUCCESS

I have developed a formula or an outline or a checklist of sorts, to help make sure I cover everything in a session. There are seven major sections or phases, and each has certain things to accomplish when we're in that stage or phase.

This structure is laid out below for an overview, and then we'll talk about each individual component and fill in the details as we go. This is my session structure, and you may find it useful with your clients.

PRETALK
Welcome
Find Out Experience with Hypnosis
How They Heard about You
Positive Reinforcement
Explain Hypnosis
Answer Questions
Collect Payment
Complete Forms
Convincers

ASSESSMENT
Intake / Interview
Specific Tools

INDUCTION
Eye Fixation or Eye Closure
Progressive Relaxation
Autogenic Experience
Creative Visualization Tailored to Learning Style

DEEPENER
Number Count
Ratify Hypnosis
A Comment on the "Sleep Command"

SUGGESTIVE THERAPY
Indirect Suggestion
Transitional Deepening Suggestion
Ego-Strengthening
Direct Suggestion
Hypnotic Phenomena
Post-Hypnotic Suggestion

AWAKENING
Orientation to Surroundings
Energize
Direct Suggestion to Open Eyes

AFTER THE SESSION
Check for Time Distortion
Review Suggestions
Schedule Next Appointment

PRETALK
Welcome
Complete Forms
Collect Payment
Find Out Experience with Hypnosis
How They Heard about You
Positive Reinforcement
Explain Hypnosis
Answer Questions
Convincers

Let's talk a little bit about the structure of a hypnosis session. I believe that script writing/reading for the client begins before they even come into the therapy office. It begins during the pre-talk and the assessment, whether that's on the phone when they make the appointment, or in the waiting room during introductions.

Is this scripting? In a sense, yes. I have certain things that I say and questions I ask to every client. It's the "welcome" script, or "welcome" patter, if you will. And then I listen to the client's responses, and take notes—sometimes just mentally, but usually I literally jot some ideas down on paper. These notes give me information about the client, their expectations and their goals, that I can use during the session to help them achieve what they want. And, this leads to session success.

The following is an outline of the structure of a basic hypnosis pre-talk. When practicing hypnosis it is important to work in concert with a client, observing and responding in time to the client's experience. For this reason, I have not provided complete word-for-word scripts, which often leads to a one-size-fits-all communication, and this is rarely successful. Instead, this is an outline, and then we will discuss the individual components and some sample patter you may find useful and adaptable for your clients.

Pre-Talk:

Welcome, I am glad you are here.

Have you ever experienced hypnosis before?

> *Yes—Great, I love to work with people who know how to use hypnosis.*

> *No—Great, I love to work with people who are learning new skills.*

How did you hear about us?

Let me take a moment to explain a few things about hypnosis:

Hypnosis is both safe and natural; everyone is hypnotized each day, with or without a hypnotist.

For example: Highway hypnosis, concentration, resting before sleep.

Do you have any questions?

Consent: *Do you have any other questions, or are you ready to begin our hypnosis session?*

> **Welcome**
> **Complete Forms**
> **Collect Payment**
> ***Find out Experience with Hypnosis***
> ***How they Heard about You***

We begin with the pleasantries in the waiting room. This appears to be the standard idle chit-chat that everyone expects when they enter an office. But, it's also your patter. You have an agenda—to have specific questions answered, so you can build a great suggestive script for the client—and so you want to make sure that you cover everything during the 'casual discussion.'

> *Hi, welcome! I'm Richard Nongard, and I'll be your hypnotherapist today. Come in, sit down. Here's some standard paperwork to fill out, just like other offices, and you can get started on that now.*

I use the following statement when I give them the initial intake and assessment forms to complete:

> *When you called we discussed the fee of $259 for the three sessions. As you fill out these forms, I will get your receipt. Are you going to be paying with a check, cash or a credit card? (wait for answer) Okay, I will process that now while you're completing the paperwork.*

I give them a few minutes to knock out some of the forms, then return with the receipt, and ask a standard casual question:

> *Have you ever been hypnotized before?*

If they respond, yes, that's fantastic—it lets me know they are familiar with the process, and theoretically I will have less explaining to do and we can get on with the session more quickly.

However, we should never assume, and so I'll follow up with a statement question:

Obviously it was a good experience?

The main question I'm trying find the answer to is, if they saw a different hypnotist before, why are they coming to me, now? Did they have a bad experience, did they or the other hypnotist move away, or did they hear something wonderful about me personally? Their answer to the above question will shed light on their expectations, which is useful when scripting.

From here they will explain either, yes, it was great, and they want more (positive expectations that they will succeed at their goals today), or no, either the previous session didn't work or there was an issue with that therapist or whatever.

Positive Reinforcement
Explain Hypnosis
Answer Questions

Even if they say they've had a bad experience with hypnosis, they are still here in my office. This must mean that they do believe that hypnosis can help them, and so their expectations are still positive, even if circumstantial. I will commend them on making the decision to try again to reach their goals.

I'm really glad that you've decided to come here and use hypnosis for this issue. I'm sure you will do very well.

I may ask a few more questions about their prior experience, and answer them with pre-talk explanation patter, perhaps noting that:

Every hypnotist has a different approach, and I think we'll get along great together.

If the client answers no to the original question—no, they have never been hypnotized before—then we're off and running with full pre-talk explanation, commending them for being ready to make important life changes—

I'm really glad that you've decided to come here and learn how to use hypnosis. I'm sure you will do very well!

—and informing them of what hypnosis is like and what they should expect to experience.

Note the positive reinforcement in both examples above. This statement is very important:

I'm really glad that you've decided to come here and learn how to use hypnosis. I'm sure you will do very well.

That is a suggestion, and the beginning of a compound suggestion. In hypnosis, the pre-talk, induction, and the deepener work together creating compound suggestions, meaning that one suggestion follows and builds upon the last. I told them I was glad they were here, and then I gave them the first suggestion: *I'm sure you will do very well.* Magic words.

Convincers

Now, pre-talk, in many situations, has been thought to be the time when the hypnotist does a lot of flashy convincer demonstrations. I don't do very many convincers with my clients in clinical hypnotherapy from that perspective, simply because my clients already made an appointment for hypnosis so I'm assuming that they want me to hypnotize them, even if this is their very first session. Of course some clients may be a bit hesitant or nervous at first, and a convincer can break the ice and help them realize that hypnosis is painless and simple.

However, most who show up are motivated with a goal and an agenda, and they are ready for anything, so I rarely need to do any "convincers" to convince them that hypnotherapy is valid or that hypnosis is the best course of action for them. I can safely assume that they are already willing to be hypnotized and that they already assume that there will be tremendous benefits from coming to my office for a hypnosis therapy session.

So, while I don't generally do flashy convincer demonstrations, I do use convincers, in context of the pre-talk and assessment. Let me explain.

Clients who come in for weight loss, for example, want to know, "How can hypnosis help me to lose weight?"

In this situation, I might do the lemon drop convincer. I have them close their eyes and:

> *Imagine there is a lemon drop candy in your hand, and you are going to eat the imaginary candy, and when the imaginary candy touches your tongue, the sugary exterior gives way to that sour interior.*

And then I have them open their eyes and describe for me what they experienced and any changes they noticed during that process.

And almost all of them say, "Wow, I salivated" or "Gee, I could feel it in my hand" or "Amazing, I could actually taste the sour and the sweet!" And I explain to them that hypnosis can help them to, for example, lose weight, because the mind actually responds physically to the things that it creates mentally.

The implication is that if I can produce, with an imaginary candy, a physical response like salivation, then in clinical hypnotherapy I can produce a physical response of being able to effectively lose weight through suggestion and through new patterns of learning that are established during a hypnosis session.

So, part of the clinical suggestions that I give actually begin during the pre-talk and assessment process, when I provide some examples of how hypnosis works.

Here's more of the patter I often use during the pre-talk:

Before you experience trance, I want to share a few things with you.

My language here is very important. *Before you experience trance* makes the assumption that *they are going to* experience trance. Experiencing trance is something that they can and will do. This sets up success.

During hypnosis, I'm not the one in control— you are in control. All hypnosis is actually self-hypnosis; I'm just a helpful guide. It's kind of like you're driving a car, and I'm the guy sitting next to you with the map, and I'm telling you which way you can go. You're driving, and you don't have to listen to me if you don't want to, but if you follow my directions we will get to the destination you want.

I use these types of similes and metaphors simply to educate my clients as to what the hypnotic process is going to be like. These are some of the 'magic words' in my pre-talk script. They serve to put the unfamiliar concept of hypnosis into terms and concepts that the client can relate to, and this understanding breeds comfort, acceptance, rapport and trust.

During the assessment process of the first session, people often ask, "What is hypnosis going to be like, or feel like?" In response I may use a simple convincer.

> *Hypnosis is not a magical or mystical state of sixth dimension, but rather a natural state of focused concentration. Let me show you. Go ahead and close your eyes. Now count to five—one, two, three, four, five—and now open your eyes.*

And they do this: close their eyes—count one, two, three, four, five—then pop open their eyes—and then look at me funny, as if waiting for the punch line. I explain:

> *That's it—all there is to it. That's exactly what hypnosis feels like. You are always going to be able to hear my voice. You will always know where you are. You'll always be able to respond to me or open your eyes at any point if you want to. Hypnosis feels exactly like that. It's like you're relaxing in a chair and I'm talking to you and you're listening to me, just like right now.*
>
> *You can let yourself pay close attention to my words or you can let your conscious mind drift and dream and wander while the subconscious mind focuses on the experience.*

During our session, you might hear me reading some stories or even suggestions that I've written. It's perfectly okay for me to do this because I want to make sure that we cover everything that's important to you and for you to learn during our session.

So, if you hear me reading a story, it will be a story that will benefit your learning. And if you hear me reading some suggestions, this is to make certain that we don't miss anything that is important.

That, by the way, gives us permission to feel confident going into the session with the microphone, with the papers in hand and simply reading to them some of the notes/suggestions we have been jotting down during this chat.

This simple experience right in the waiting room takes the mystery away from hypnosis. It lets people see that hypnosis is natural phenomena, a process they engage in each and every day.

Hypnosis is like the first five minutes of sleep. You know that you can get up if you wanted to, but it feels so good to relax that you'll just continue as you are.

Or, I let people know:

Hypnosis is a lot like being in a classroom with a boring professor, and you space out, and you think about whatever you want to, but when exam time comes you still pass the test.

These analogies, these teaching experiences that I provide my clients in the form of convincers are things that I've pretty much committed to memory (scripted), and I use them time after time with my clients.

Again, they provide easy explanation, which leads to a sense of comfort, and therefore builds rapport, which leads to trust, which is essential for a solid therapeutic relationship.

> *People who learn to use hypnosis find it even easier to experience success. You are in control of your experience, and at any time you can go into a deeper trance if that feels right for you, or you can remain in a lighter trance, and focus on your learnings.*

My suggestion here is that they are going to enter a trance, and they will enter at either a light level or a deep level, but either way they're going to do well.

This knowledge (via suggestion during explanation) takes a lot of conscious stress off their mind, because a lot of people worry about whether or not they are going to do well with this, or whether or not they will understand it, or whether or not they will be able to go into a deep enough level of trance.

For most things, other than hypnosurgery, hypnoanesthesia, and some advanced pain management techniques, the trance depth level of the client experience is not really related or correlated to outcome. Clients are just as likely to experience success with most things regardless of trance depth, so I want them to know it's perfectly okay to experience this the way they want to experience it.

> *Hypnosis is a perfectly safe and natural process you have engaged in on a daily basis throughout your life. The word hypnosis actually comes from the Greek word sleep, but you're never going to be asleep, just relaxed. You will be able to use the*

creative and intuitive part of the mind to replace old ideas or patterns with new thoughts and ideas.

And so I believe that good hypnotherapy comes from good language, which begins by being prepared to answer the client's questions and help them to understand what hypnosis is going to be like, during the pre-talk and assessment phase.

Now, do I have all these statements scripted out word for word on paper in front of me? No, not at all. But I might have keywords jotted down, as a reminder of some convincer or explanation stories I can refer to and decide to use if they fit the context of a question they ask.

And when the paperwork is complete—contact information, informed consent release, assessment questionnaire, learning style assessment—we move into the therapy office, ready to complete the assessment process and begin to make changes.

ASSESSMENT
Intake/Interview
Specific Tools

Up to now we have discussed the language used during the pre-talk to help the client understand and become comfortable with the concept of hypnosis, and to build rapport and trust with the hypnotist. These things increase the odds of session success dramatically.

The formal assessment process is equally important, because it helps you to create the proper individualized interventions, or suggestions, to help the client achieve the goal at hand with greater short- and long-term success.

For example, let's say your standard quit smoking script that you downloaded off the Internet uses the aversion strategy: cigarettes are gross; the smell makes you nauseous, holding a cigarette is like holding a deadly snake; they taste like the vilest thing you can think of, and so forth.

Now, this may be an effective strategy for a few clients you see, at least in the short run—but it will not work for everyone.

If you only have one smoking cessation script—that you use with every client—you may help them quit initially, but they may not experience long-term success.

The client who is terribly uncomfortable in social situations and uses smoking as a comfort tool may decide next week or next month that the nasty taste (caused by your aversion therapy) is worth the risk, just so they can remain calm and in control when at a party.

The client who smokes to help curb their appetite may decide that remaining thin before a big event is worth the price of a carton of cigarettes.

And a client who is helped to quit without any other health-related suggestions, such as with nutritional and fitness concepts, may develop weight problems within a few months after quitting.

However, before you assist a client for weight loss and suggest that they start jogging or join an aerobics class, do an assessment and make sure they do not have a health condition such as asthma or knee problems that would preclude them from engaging in these kinds of activities. (I know this may sound like basic common sense, but one would also think restaurants would not need to advertise that coffee is hot.)

Consider the client who comes in for fear of public speaking. You can do all the self-confidence and 'circle of power' work you want—but if their underlying problem is that they are uncomfortable with their weight, or speech problems such as a lisp, or their old clothes, or a birthmark or whatever else—you likely won't see the kinds of results you want unless and until you integrate suggestions to help overcome these other specific areas as well.

And, you won't know they exist unless you ask.

This is why it is also so important to be flexible, adaptable, and well-versed with creating suggestive sessions—and why assessment is so valuable to success. So take the extra few minutes to get more details from the client about the specific issue they bring to the table.

Ask casual common-sense questions—both on the intake form and in the verbal interview—and take notes on the key points, so you will be able to integrate specific, individualized additional concepts (social confidence, weight maintenance, acceptance, etc.) into your primary goal therapeutic suggestions.

When completing the assessment process, it is helpful to use an outline, to make sure you don't forget to ask important questions.

There are several intake/assessment tools you can use to

help you cover the basics, but no matter how lengthy they are, asking follow-up questions (verbal interview/discussion) is vitally important so there is no misinterpretation. For more information on intake and assessment tools, see Appendices A and B.

The more you know up front about your clients' situational and emotional positions on the subject at hand, the more you can help them be prepared for surprise and even routine challenges by implementing specific targeted suggestions into their sessions, and the better equipped they will be to avoid relapse.

Other things to consider—and evaluate during your assessment—are the terms and words you use during induction, deepening, and metaphorical suggestions.

Many hypnotists, including myself, often use descriptions involving moving up or down staircases, climbing mountains, or drifting deeper into soft feather pillow beds.

These concepts may sound rather innocuous, but to the client who is afraid of heights or allergic to feathers, the use of these words may create instant tension and resistance, and even bring them right out of trance.

If you want your client to visualize a relaxing place, either let them generate their own or make sure to offer several alternatives for them to choose from. If you only suggest "a relaxing place, such as on the beach at the ocean," and they are afraid of water or have had a bad experience at the beach in the past, you may cause more stress than relaxation.

Have a brief discussion with the client—during your assessment pre-talk—about the techniques and concepts you plan to use, and ask if those concepts sound relaxing to them—or not.

Or better yet, during the relaxation process, encourage the client to generate their own peaceful scenery or place they enjoy and would like to 'escape' to or relax at, and use their choice—and they will be happy and even more willing to follow your suggestions.

Flexibility and adaptability on the part of the hypnotist is so vitally essential for facilitating long-term success. Customizing patter for your clients to insure you are meeting their needs is essential, because again, every client is different.

Richard K. Nongard

INDUCTION
Eye Fixation or Eye Closure
Progressive Relaxation
Autogenic Experience
Creative Visualization Tailored to Learning Style

The next area where good planning and effective patter are essential is during the actual hypnotic induction. The induction is the formal process of guiding a person into a state of relaxation—or concentration or creativity or focus or open-mindedness or trance—generally the theta level of brain functioning, where they are open to new learnings.

There are hundreds if not thousands of different inductions and induction styles to choose from, and on my website, SubliminalScience.com, you can actually download some scripts for inducing clinical hypnosis, for free.

At this stage in my career, I use a variety of different inductions, generally depending on my assessment of the individual client. But when I started, I had one script that I practiced and practiced and used with everyone, until I was convinced that it would really work. (Yes, that confidence issue you may struggle with is common to all new hypnotists.)

If you are a new hypnotist, I think it's perfectly okay to use a detailed induction script and bring it into your therapy sessions to make sure that you follow a process that will actually be effective and work. Is it acceptable to sit and read the induction word for word directly from the pages? It's not the best plan for the long run, but in the beginning, yes, you can.

The caution here is that while you're reading you also want to make sure to keep one eye on your client as much as the paper, paying attention to their responses to your words. Are they are following your instructions? You can pause in your reading, and you must also assess their relaxation progress so you can adjust your pacing and pausing if necessary, give them time to respond, or encourage them more intently.

I've written a book titled, *Inductions and Deepeners: Styles and Approaches for Effective Hypnosis*, and in it there are about seventeen different inductions, plus several more deepeners. Each induction has its place with different types of clients, and different hypnotists simply tend to prefer or be more comfortable with one particular style or another.

Choosing an induction style is rather like car shopping. When you're young and desperate, you'll take any car you can get. If it runs, drives and stops, and does the job of getting you to and from where you need to be, it's good enough. When we're older and have more finances, and more responsibilities to consider, we become more selective. We want a car that is comfortable, either around town or for long trips. It needs to have enough seats, if we have children or friends to taxi around. Perhaps it should be a mini-van with easy-open push-button side doors. Or maybe it needs leather seats that are easy to clean. When possible, if we had unlimited funds, we would select a comfortable, functional 'daily driver' *and* a flashy sports car, *and* perhaps a sedan cruiser or a tough four-wheel drive, so that we can always go anywhere we want at any time.

There are dozens if not hundreds of possible styles and options to choose from when shopping for an automobile, and we seek to find the one that is the best fit for our personal wants and needs. Choosing induction scripts is very similar. We should test drive and become familiar with several different styles, so that we can discover what we like best (our daily driver), and also know what options are available for best meeting the needs of our individual clients.

Personally, I primarily use a progressive muscle relaxation (PMR) induction combined with autogenic training techniques with most of my clients. Autogenic techniques simply ask a client to create sensations (warmth, heaviness, etc.) in their body. And while the concept and approach of PMR is generally the same from client to client—controlled breathing, muscle attention group focus—I still customize the content for each client.

Here is a sample of how I might script out a PMR induction. The entire induction is not here word-for-word, but I have written down some parts completely that I may actually read or just glance at now and then, and others are reminder notes for things I have committed to memory but do not want to leave out.

Induction

The easiest way to experience hypnosis is by just letting yourself follow the instructions I give.

You do not have to try to be hypnotize; it is a natural state you will easily be able to experience.

It is okay during our session to adjust for comfort, swallow, or move.

In fact, these things will not disturb you; they will actually help you to become more comfortable, and relax even further.

And should a plane overhead make noise, or a car outside of the office, or if someone like the UPS or mailman comes in, none of these things will disturb you either.

In fact, they will simply assure you that you are exactly where you are supposed to be and doing exactly what you need to be doing to take care of yourself.

Eye Fixation or Eye Closure

Examples: Light source, spot on wall, or simply close eyes if comfortable and ready.

Progressive Muscle Relaxation:

As you breathe in and out, noticing your breathing already becoming smooth and rhythmic, notice what it feels like to relax.

And anywhere in the body you sense tension, just let those muscles relax.

Pay attention to the muscles of the face, the eyes, the brow and the jaw. Let those muscles relax.

And now, let your chin fall towards your chest, bringing a sense of relaxation to the shoulders, neck, and back.

Arms

Hands

And do not worry or be concerned if to this point your mind has been racing or thinking or even analyzing this process; after all, this is what minds do, they think. We will get to how to still or relax the mind in a moment.

Autogenic training:

> Now focus on your hands and say the word "heavy," and as you say the word "heavy," let those hands become heavy.
>
> And now think of the word "warmth," and let your hands sense the feeling of warmth.
>
> And say to yourself, "my hands are warm and heavy" ... "my hands are warm and heavy" ... and just let those hands be warm and heavy.
>
> And now focus on the muscles of the back, buttocks, and thighs.
>
> Feel the sense of relaxation through the thighs, calves, and into the ankles and little muscles of the feet, even the tiny muscles in the toes.
>
> Perfect.

Autogenic training: Feet

Body Scan:

> Now notice how your body feels, the heart rate slow and smooth, and your breathing smooth and rhythmic.
>
> And even though you know you could move your heavy hands and feet at any time, it feels so good to let go and relax that you can now find it easier to just let your body become even more relaxed.

Creative Visualization:

Now as easily as you can relax the body, you can relax the mind.

One way is to do this through creative visualization. Imagine yourself outside on a perfect day, in either a beautiful place you have been before, a place you would like to go, or even a place of your own creation.

And focus your attention now on the clear blue sky and a single white puffy cloud....

This is an example of the kind of induction script I might carry into the therapy office with me. It's an outline with a few paragraphs of patter. I probably don't need to use it at all, because at this stage in my career I have most induction language memorized, but it's always good to have a cheat-sheet so I don't get distracted and lose my place or forget any specific component that I want to include.

Sometimes I'll even use a pen or pencil and check a section off once I've completed it, both so I don't accidentally repeat myself and so I don't skip anything. You wouldn't think this could happen, but if you are constantly looking up at the client to watch their responses and back down at your paper, it's quite possible to get jumbled.

Now, if you recall, above in the assessment process I discussed using different tools, and one that I use with every single client no matter what issue they want to address is the *Nongard Assessment of Primary Representation Systems*, which assesses their learning style. I want to know, are they an audio, visual, or a kinesthetic learner? Once I have determined their strong suit, I try to match an induction script to their learning style.

Let's look at some examples of how we may use an **auditory language learning style** in an induction:

> *As you relax each muscle of your body, you begin to listen to your own thoughts, hearing each word as I speak with both the conscious and the subconscious mind.*
>
> *As your body relaxes, your mind can relax also, and you can turn up the volume of this stillness or relaxation, enjoying the process of entering trance and learning hypnosis.*

This is an example of using auditory-focused language patterns to help a person enter trance.

With **visual learning styles** for induction, I may say something like:

> *As you continue to relax each and every muscle of the body, create a mental picture in your mind of a clear blue sky, and imagine yourself looking up at that clear blue sky on a perfect day. Perhaps in a beautiful and relaxing place that you've been before, or perhaps in a perfect place that you'd like to go, or a place that you've simply created in your own mind.*

This is a permissive structure that allows the client to create the visual imagery that is important to them.

The third learning style is kinesthetic, meaning tactile, physical sensations, or hands-on. The kinesthetic person learns by feeling things, and this scripting style actively engages them in the process. Here's an example of **kinesthetic induction language:**

As you relax, feeling the muscles loosen and your hands becoming heavier, you can feel the process of entering trance.

This is an amazing skill each of us possesses; feeling the sensation of heaviness in each muscle as it becomes loose allows you to experience an even deeper level of trance.

The learning style assessment allows me to carefully craft my induction language choices to be more consistent with the client's personal style.

If I am in doubt about my client's learning style, or if I am addressing a group, I make sure to include information from all the senses, or to be artfully vague. For example, I use the term "fluffy pillow" in place of "feather bed" because it is equally visual and kinesthetic—and I recommend that you always do so. If you use this kind of visualization, why take chances on complications? Simple word choices can make all the difference to the client's state of relaxation and concentration.

So in summary, select an induction style that you like, that you are comfortable with, and that has proven to be effective with your clients. Sketch it out on paper if you don't have it memorized, and make notes on whether your client is more auditory, kinesthetic or visually oriented, and jot down examples of patter—metaphors, phrases, and so on—that you can use in the induction language to help aid in a more personal, effective induction.

DEEPENER
Number Count
Ratify Hypnosis
A Comment on the "Sleep Command"

My favorite deepener is a simple number count with fractionation, and I'll share with you some examples of how I do that. Fractionation brings a person to a deeper level of trance, and then brings them up a little bit, and then bringing them back down to an even deeper level.

You might be wondering why, of all the many deepening techniques available, do I use a simple number count in clinical hypnosis? Purely because it's easy, and it is consistent with the majority of my clients' expectations. Most people only know maybe three things about a hypnotist: 1) they can make you cluck like a chicken, 2) they use a swinging pocket watch to trance you out, and 3) they count backwards, and it does something magical.

Ahem. So, they've heard that a hypnotist counts, and so I use these magic words and count for them, backwards, from ten to one:

Ten, nine, eight, seven... You're doing so well.

Eight, seven, six, five. Perfect. Just continue to double that sensation of relaxation.

Seven, six, five, four... All the way down. You're doing so well.

> And continue to relax every muscle in your body and your mind as well, doubling the sensation with each number.
>
> Five, four, three, two, one... Perfect. You're doing so well. Simply let go completely.
>
> Three, two, one, zero.

This is a very short and simple count-down deepener, but it also uses fractionation because I keep going back up to a higher number as I come down again.

Also, I count backwards not from ten down to one, but from ten to zero, because when I hit zero most folks usually drop off into an even deeper level of hypnotic trance than if I stop at one.

Having ready-made deepener scripts can be very useful. You can read from them on paper, or simply memorize these short phrases or processes.

Here's how you can add **visualization to a number count deepener**:

> Imagine yourself at the top of a majestic flight of stairs. As you step down each stair, you are doubling the sensation of relaxation. Ten, moving down, nine, holding the stately hand rail, eight, relaxing, doubling the relaxation, seven.... and so forth.

You can also be very **kinesthetic with deepening**, with or without counting.

> Breathe in with your eyes closed, let your chin fall gently down to your chest, and simply relax. Feel your muscles begin to loosen and become limp. And with each breath, in and out, smooth and rhythmic, allow yourself to feel an even deeper state of trance.

The following is a slightly expanded **fractionation number count deepening script** outline that I use, with ego strengthening, usually after a PMR induction. You can see how the additional patter used between the numbers could be **easily modified** to include more visual, auditory, or kinesthetic language as necessary, depending on the individual client.

Customization = Magic Words.

> You've done very well, allowing both the body and mind to relax. And so now I'm going to count backwards from ten to zero, and with each number, simply let your body relax even more.

> And as your body relaxes, you will find that your mind is also relaxing, doubling the sensation of relaxation with each number.

> Ten, nine, eight... Perfect.

> And as I count... Seven, six, five... With the conscious mind you may be wondering, is it okay to count so quickly?

But the subconscious mind doesn't wonder. It simply enjoys the process of doubling the sensation of relaxation with each number.

In fact, it doesn't even matter what numbers I count...

Eight, seven, six, five...

All that matters is you follow the process, doubling the sensation of relaxation with each number.

Six, five, four, three... Good.

As you relax, go deeper into trance. Three, two, one...

And you can drift as quickly into trance as you want to, or slowly enjoying the feeling of entering a deep trance, but doubling the sensation of relaxation with each number.

Three, two, one, zero... Perfect.

Now, a lot of hypnotists ask me, how come you double the relaxation? What about making it 10,000 times deeper or a billion times deeper? Well, simply because doubling is a concept that is easy for people to understand.

With every breath, every time you exhale, your relaxation doubles.

Breathe in slowly, all the way in... and now, all the way out... Relaxing even further. Excellent.

They can understand conceptually what 'twice as deep, doubling the sensation of relaxation' feels like. When we start coming up with 100 times deeper or a billion times stronger, they don't really know what this means or how much it is—and we don't want them wondering or edging into anxiety over whether what their feeling is technically in line with whatever number scale I'm throwing out.

I've found that 'doubling the sensation' is something that both the conscious and the subconscious mind can easily listen and respond to, and so that's what I use.

Ratify Hypnosis

People who come to your office and have never experienced hypnosis before are often unsure of what hypnosis is. They know they want change, but this is all very new to them. So, in addition to providing clear pre-talk explaining hypnosis before the session, I also want to do two other things, near the end of my induction or deepener.

First, I want them to note, both physically and mentally, that change has occurred. What this does is prove in the client's own mind that something is happening. The logical outcome is that if something is happening, then something *will* happen.

Second, I want to tell them when they are hypnotized, so they will know and can stop questioning the process with their conscious mind.

The two strategies I use to ratify trance are:

1) feedback from the client that they have experienced hypnotic phenomena,

and

2) direct suggestion.

I usually combine these two, but it is perfectly acceptable to use only one or the other.

Let me share with you how I use manifestation of hypnotic phenomena as a way of ratifying trance. During my induction, I almost always use an autogenic suggestion that my client will feel like their hands are becoming warm and heavy. I have the client state out loud several times,

"My hands are warm and heavy."
(repeating) *"My hands are warm and heavy."*

As we continue and go into the deepener, (or sometimes following the deepener), I tell them,

You are doing perfect, creating new experiences.

Then I ask them:

Are you able to feel warmth or heaviness (notice it is an option—not all clients feel all things) *in your hands?*

They always answer in the affirmative.

This simple process causes clients to say to themselves, "Wow, I felt change; I must be going into hypnosis!"

Depending on the client, I may use a different form of hypnotic phenomena to have them ratify trance so they will know they are going into hypnosis. As I write this passage, I'm thinking about a new client I had just this morning who had never seen nor really even heard of hypnosis before. He came only because a friend had recommended my services, and he trusted his friend. Since he was a former police detective, I knew intuitively that he would need a little convincing, so I used the "sticky hand" bit you may have seen a stage hypnotist use. However, instead of using it for its comedic value, I used it as a proof or convincer to the client that he was hypnotized. I combined this with the autogenic technique described above.

As he relaxed, I said to him:

As your hands rest at your side, warm and heavy, so very heavy and so very warm, you can notice that even though the conscious mind knows you can lift your hands, your subconscious mind has created such a heaviness in those hands that when you try to lift them you find they become heavier and heavier and impossible to lift. In fact, the harder you try to lift them, the stucker they become!

Then I immediately went into a transitional deepener:

And now double the sensation of relaxation, through your entire mind and body, doubling the sensation of relaxation with each number, 5-4-3-2-1-0....

Convincers become even more powerful (and more likely to work) when used during the deepener or induction, rather than during the pre-talk. They convince the client they are in fact hypnotized, and that makes the entire session much easier.

Regardless whether I have done the things listed above or not in a session, I always use direct suggestion at the end of my deepener to tell people they are in fact hypnotized. I want clients to know they are hypnotized, that this is what they came for, and this is how it feels.

This is very important, and the reason is simple: If I make the direct suggestion that they are hypnotized, they will take action on this belief. The action they will take is to change or follow my other suggestions.

Here is what I say:

This is the point we call hypnosis. A state you have created, a state of focused attention or deep relaxation, but most importantly hypnosis is a state of creativity and learning, allowing you to have new experiences and accomplish new things. Although never asleep, deeply relaxed. Listening to my words and going deeper....

A Comment on the "Sleep Command"

Those who have watched a stage hypnotist often wonder, how did he get them to go back into trance so quickly throughout the show, just by yelling the word "sleep?" What happens here in clinical hypnosis with the patter above is essentially the same thing that a stage hypnotist does when he gives the "sleep command." In stage hypnosis, the performer tells the members of the show when they are hypnotized, and that anytime he or she gives the command (often the word "Sleep!"), they will return to this very place or state of relaxation.

The principle is the same in clinical hypnosis, even though most hypnotherapists rarely use the word "sleep." When I tell my clients they are in hypnosis, and they have ascribed the role of hypnotist to me, they will act as if—and in fact be—hypnotized when I tell them they are.

SUGGESTIVE THERAPY
Indirect Suggestion
Transitional Deepening Suggestion
Ego-Strengthening
Direct Suggestion
Hypnotic Phenomena
Post-Hypnotic Suggestion

Suggestive therapy is the part of the session in which you directly effect change, and there are many ways to go about it. Nonetheless, I've found that the following order works best for me.

Indirect Suggestion

Following trance ratification, I provide indirect suggestion for further relaxation and beginning learnings in the form of a metaphor, story, or parable.

Milton Erickson's theory was that the mind is very literal, and that when it hears a story, no matter if the subject is familiar or not, the subconscious mind sees the story from a literal perspective and can find some way to make relative sense out of it. And so, Ericksonian hypnotherapy uses a lot of indirect metaphor storytelling as a way of structuring and creating suggestions designed to be helpful to a client.

Personally, I'm a firm believer that metaphors and stories should be easily understood by the client without effort. For example, let's say I'm a hypnotherapist in Kansas or Nebraska, and if I were to have a client come in who has never been to a real beach—because the ocean is at least a two-day drive from there—

they likely can't relate to the feeling of walking on the beach and feeling sand between their toes or the warm sun beating on their back with the seagulls cawing in the air.

So, if I'm going to tell a story or create a relaxing visualization scenario, it needs to be one that is understood by my client—perhaps a meadow or field of flowers, or even a swimming pool rather than the ocean—something that they can relate to that won't cause distracting confusion due to a lack of experience with the subject.

> As you continue to relax, I'm going to read for you a parable that can teach a lot to our subconscious mind about hypnosis.
>
> It goes like this: The stream, swiftly running through a beautiful valley, did reproach the great river for flowing so slowly. Said the river, "We two the morning dawn shall see, you quickly, I slowly, both fall into the sea."

In this particular example, this very short parable is not related to smoking cessation or anxiety or pain management or anything else; its design is to help a person understand the hypnotic process better. But I could give a parable, a story, or a metaphor to help with these things.

For example, here's one for weight loss:

> Consider the gardener who tends to the vegetables, and as the seeds are planted, and the plants germinate, and the flowers give way to fruit, and that fruit becomes larger and healthier and stronger...

> *The fruit never has to ask gardener, "How much nutrition from the soil should I use? How much rain from the sky must I drink?"*
>
> *Intuitively the perfect fruit of life knows what is needed by listening to Mother Nature.*
>
> *And in this same way, you instinctively know how much nutrition you should consume, and that when your hunger or thirst is quenched, it's time to stop.*

With addicted clients, I might use this patter:

> *And as you relax, I am going to share many ideas with you. Some will be direct suggestion, and others perhaps stories of some kind. In fact, I am reminded now of a story about a man named Jim...*

I will then tell or read a story, in this case the story about Jim is appropriate for addiction and is recounted in the *Big Book of Alcoholics Anonymous*—a great book with numerous stories about change, many of which are adaptable to situations other than addiction.

I also recommend that every hypnotist pick up Cory Hammond's book, often referred to by hypnotists as "the big red book," which is actually titled, *The Handbook of Hypnotic Suggestions and Metaphors*.

Transitional Deepening Suggestion

Following the indirect suggestion metaphor or story, it might be time for a transitional deepener.

Rarely does a person just fall into a deep trance and stay there the whole time. Instead, they usually kind of drift and dream, floating up and down and back and forth during a session.

You can use a transitional deepener any time you think it's necessary. Personally, I almost always do one after a metaphor, story, or parable, before I proceed with direct suggestion. This is a deepening and ego-strengthening suggestion that helps the client become even more receptive or open to the next suggestions that follow. It is very similar to the trance ratification deepening suggestion.

What are the magic words? I simply tell them (again) they are now (or still) experiencing a state of hypnosis. They can let go of the conscious mind's critical faculty and allow themselves to simply go on with the process, the subconscious process of experiencing hypnosis.

> *Notice now that you feel differently at this moment than you did a few minutes ago or even when you walked in the door. And notice how although you know you could open your eyes it feels so good to relax, then when you try to open them they become even more comfortable and become locked down tighter with relaxation. This is hypnosis, a state you have created, and a state of learning and creativity...*

Or:

> *You have created a wonderful state of relaxation for yourself. Perfect. And, this is what trance feels like.*

You can hear my words, and you know you're safe, for you have created this place of perfect concentration. It is in this state that you can access the part of the mind that is most creative, and easily learn the skills of hypnosis which follow, to enhance your success.

This lets them know that not only are they hypnotized, but that they can use this state to their benefit. It reassures them that they are safe, and it lets them know that we are, at this moment, engaged in the process of hypnosis—and from here we can begin with suggestive therapy language.

Another example of a simple transitional deepener is:

As you continue falling either quickly or slowly into trance, allow each breath to take you to an even deeper level of trance. In, and out... Slowly breathing, and with each breath deepening your experience of trance.

If I notice that the client is struggling a bit with complete relaxation, I may even say something like:

I can see that you're using both your conscious and your subconscious mind to focus on this process and you can allow yourself to even go deeper by simply letting go of any conscious opposition and simply embracing the process with your subconscious mind that allows you to learn these things and to use that creative and intuitive part of the mind.

We can use these transitional deepeners to deepen trance at any point during the hypnotic process.

Ego Strengthening

Following the indirect suggestion and transitional deepener suggestion, I usually use an ego strengthener.

I think it's important to affirm to clients that they are doing well—that this is the process that they came in for and that they are going through it just fine and dandy.

> *I teach a lot of people how to use hypnosis, and you're doing so well. And as you allow yourself to enjoy this experience you know that this is the right way to help you be successful.*

That is an ego strengthener; it affirms that they have made the right choice and that the are engaged in the process correctly.

Again, this construct of magic words allows them to give up any conscious worries about whether or not they are doing it right. There is not a right way or a wrong way to do hypnosis, and as long as my client is engaged in the process, whichever way they are experiencing trance is the right way.

> *A person does not have to have their eyes closed, or even be relaxed in order to experience hypnosis. They simply need to be able to access the creative part of the mind where awareness itself is created. And in accessing that part of the mind, new learnings can take place that can help them be successful at any issue that has brought them to the office.*

Direct Suggestion

Direct suggestion is exactly what it sounds like: a suggestion from me that directly tells them how they are going to feel, how they are going to respond, how they are going to experience or interpret the events of the present and of the future.

For example, let's say I'm working with a cigarette smoker who smokes a lot of cigarettes in the morning because they believe nicotine gives them energy, kind of like caffeine does, that they need to face the day.

I may give them a direct suggestion that:

> *From this point forward, you no longer derive your energy from nicotine, but instead find that a deep breath—filling your lungs with air and letting the oxygen infiltrate all of the cells in your body—provides you with all the energy you need to experience the day.*

An example of a direct suggestion for weight loss is:

> *From this point forward, you are able to see a dinner buffet not as an opportunity to get the most value for the money, but as an opportunity to have many different choices in the correct portion to satisfy your need for food and nutrients.*

Suggestions are best when they are used in the present tense. Good direct suggestions are:

It will be easy for you, or, *It is easy for you.*

It is easy for you now to simply eat until your hunger is satisfied, and then quit.

For weight loss clients, that simple statement is a very powerful and effective suggestion.

I want to talk now about direct suggestion and compounding. I won't give a direct suggestion to the client only once, but many times.

The first time a suggestion is received, it is fairly weak. The second time it is more effectively received, and the third time a suggestion is heard it becomes extremely effective, and this process is called compounding.

For example, I would never do a hypnosis session and tell the person, *From this point forward you are no longer a smoker,* and just leave it at that.

I want to reaffirm to them seven different times and in ten different ways that they are now a non-smoker. That they are able to derive their energy from oxygen rather than from nicotine, and that they have entered a new chapter of life, as a non-smoker. That they have successfully succeeded at accomplishing a goal. I know this because they told me they had their last cigarette before they came in the office. I want to give them the suggestion that they are now a non-smoker five, six, seven, ten times during the session, because compounding direct suggestions is more effective.

Likewise, when I do a story or metaphor and then go into direct suggestion, the direct suggestion reinforces the indirect suggestion of the previous story, for even more compounding.

Here are some examples of direct suggestions:

> *The suggestions that I'm giving you are not suggestions that come from me but rather from you. You've committed to the process of making change by taking this bold step in coming here today. So each suggestion is actually a suggestion that you've told me to make, and each suggestion that is given you'll find it easy to act on quickly, helping you to achieve your goals.*

I give the suggestion to my client that the suggestions I'm giving them are not from me but come from within them, so that they will internalize and personalize the suggestions, making them more effective.

> *You'll find success is easy for you to achieve. It's like breathing, and you know this because the first step in success has already been accomplished by you.*

The above is a generic example of a direct suggestion script. Let's plug it in with cigarette smoking specific language:

> *You'll see being a non-smoker is easy for you to achieve. It's like breathing healthy air, and you'll know this because the first step in success has already been accomplished by you by making this appointment and coming here today.*

When I make a suggestion, I tell them *why* the suggestion is going to be effective, and this also helps to avoid sounding like a fortune cookie.

What? Yes, sometimes our suggestions sound a bit like a fortune cookie—*You will no longer be a smoker. You will no longer eat Twinkies by the box. You will no longer gorge yourself on a buffet*. You will, you will, you will—as if I'm predicting the future like a fortune cookie.

So we give direct suggestions, and we compound them—give the suggestion more than once in multiple ways—and we explain why it will be beneficial.

For example:

You are now entering a new chapter of life, a chapter of life that derives energy from deep breaths of oxygen rather than from nicotine.

That's the suggestion—*You now derive your energy from oxygen rather than nicotine*. I want to reiterate that concept several times during the session. Sometimes this may seem a little redundant, but it's highly effective, as the compounding is an effective way to help people internalize and personalize the suggestions, making the change their own.

Each night you find it easier to get a deep rest using the principles of hypnosis to enter a deep and tranquil sleep. This reinvigorates your body, and so rather than deriving energy from nicotine, you are able to derive energy from proper rest, nutrition and even from taking a deep breath, letting oxygen fill your lungs and bring energy to each cell in the form of fresh air and deep breaths.

This is both a direct suggestion and a teaching suggestion, compounding the prior suggestion on energy and oxygen.

Here is an example of how I might structure a direct suggestion to help a person reframe a typical behavior related to weight loss:

As you approach a restaurant buffet, it is something you can now see as an opportunity—an opportunity to have many different healthy choices in the correct portion, and you are able to easily choose the items that are best for you, easily leaving those that are not for others to choose.

By the way, there are some key phrases to note in this direct suggestion.

You can now see the buffet as an opportunity.

Everyone loves an opportunity, an opportunity to have many different healthy food choices in the correct portion. That's a direct suggestion.

And you are able to easily choose the items that are best for you.

Everyone wants what's best. These suggestions are positive and easy to understand.

easily leaving those that are not for others to choose.

People like to feel like they're not wasting food, and so this gives them an opportunity to look at an old behavior from an entirely new perspective.

Hypnotic Phenomena

In most of my hypnosis sessions I also manifest hypnotic phenomena. This serves the purpose of letting the client know that they really are experiencing hypnosis. Using hypnotic phenomena to help a person experience success is also very effective way of building a reputation for being a good hypnotherapist.

Sometimes I use arm catalepsy so clients can physically feel the process of hypnosis—muscle rigidity and then tension relaxation. This process can be used as a metaphor for being able to discharge stress or eliminate/release old habits.

I use age regression and age progression phenomena particularly with my cigarette smokers. These concepts, by the way, are much different than past life regression (PLR).

I do not teach any religious form of hypnosis. Past life regression is really a religious practice, using hypnosis as the method of practicing religious expression, and sometimes people get past life regression mixed up with age regression. Age regression is a natural process, a trance phenomena that we all experience in everyday life.

Think about this for a minute: At your house, do you have some pictures of your family over the years? Chances are you walk by those photos every day and you don't pay too much attention to them, but every now and then you probably notice that picture of grandpa or grandma, or that picture of you when you were little, or maybe of your kids a long time ago, and you stop and pause for a moment... And suddenly it's as if you are back in that time in life again, re-experiencing that scenario.

This age regression phenomena is called revivification, and it can be extremely useful for helping a client to see things from a new perspective—when used by an experienced clinician who knows how to avoid abreaction. The client can re-experience past events and look at them from a new perspective, which can help them be able to make a decision to move forward now in a different direction.

The following is a script using age regression and age progression with cigarette smokers. It's easy for people to experience.

> *Think back now to a time when you were ten years old, a pleasant time before you ever had a cigarette.*
>
> *Imagine yourself as you were when you were ten, and see yourself as you were at that time. Now, see yourself going through the years of life having never made the choice to smoke. See yourself in places and situations in life that you experienced through life, through high school or college and even your first job.*
>
> *See yourself in these situations as if you had never made the decision to smoke, and see yourself as you were but without a cigarette, having never smoked, and in your relationships and in your houses, and in the experiences you have had.*
>
> *Now, bring yourself to today, seeing yourself as you are, a non-smoker, and imagine yourself today from the perspective of one who has never smoked. And see yourself in life over the next few weeks as one who has never smoked, and into the next year, and over the next few years, as one who has never smoked.*
>
> *They say the body can achieve whatever the mind can conceive, and you were able to create the image of experiencing the life as a non-smoker and having*

never made the choice to smoke, so it is easy for you to respond to life as one who has never smoked.

And so, seeing others smoke is not be a cue for you to smoke. You now respond to the smoking of others with ambivalence, because it is as if you have never been a smoker in the first place.

And when at home, or in your car or at work you'll find it easy to remain smoke free. These things are not cues to smoke but rather cues to feel success, happy and comfortable.

Another example of hypnotic phenomena is hypnotic anesthesia. If you work with clients in pain, using anesthesia is a great tool for helping them learn the skills of pain management or, as I usually call it, increasing comfort.

Rarely with my pain management clients do I ever use the word pain. They are already aware of their pain when they come to the office. During intake assessment and hypnosis sessions, I don't encourage the client to pay attention to their pain or discomfort level. Instead, I use the magic words of having them pay attention to their *increasing comfort* and their *ability to control comfort*.

This is an important way of reframing things and letting clients experience something new. A lot of times clients haven't been successful at quitting smoking or losing weight or managing their pain, and now they have come to us as a last resort. We want to help them succeed, and so we need to reframe or change their perspective. If they perceive us as trying to help them do exactly what they failed at before, they may become skeptical or even just give up on themselves.

In clinical hypnotherapy, when we rephrase concepts so that we are giving are positive suggestions, we are much more effective.

We don't say, "You will lose weight"—this is what they have always failed at.

Instead we say:

You now make healthier nutrition choices.

Not, "You will eat less," but:

You now eat only until your hunger is satisfied.

Posthypnotic Suggestions

In my typical session, I go from manifesting some form of hypnotic phenomena to using posthypnotic suggestions. Posthypnotic suggestions are concepts that the client is going to act upon instantly and easily following the session. These may include a number of different things related to behavior or emotional change.

For example:

Every time you see the color green, you are reminded to go ahead and take a cleansing breath and relax, knowing that you have the strength to handle whatever challenges life brings your way.

Magic Words

Or perhaps I'll just suggest that the client has the ability to re-experience hypnosis even more easily and at a deeper level of trance or comfort in the future. This last is truly positive and effective posthypnotic suggestion. Why not set it up so that your next hypnosis session with the client is entered into easily and quickly, by giving them the posthypnotic suggestion that they will respond easily to the process of hypnosis?

> *Now that you've learned the process of hypnosis, you find it easy to enter trance and be able to bring yourself back to this state of creativity and concentration that you've experienced today.*

These are quite magical words—because they help insure my client experience success in our future sessions.

Next, empower your client:

> *As you go through the rest of your day, you can feel confident of your success knowing that you have done well and have achieved your goal.*

Use the everyday world to reinforce the learning:

> *Anytime you hear a phone ring, whether it's your phone or someone else's phone, a cell phone, a house phone, an office phone or even a phone on TV, your subconscious mind is reminded of the ability you have to experience success. It brings a smile to your face, a recognition of accomplishment and a feeling of wellness and deepness from within you.*

That's a great posthypnotic suggestion.

You can also tie these concepts to colors:

> *Whenever you see the color red it serves as a reminder to you of your ability to continue to feel confident, whether it's a red drinking straw, a road sign, somebody's shirt, a tie, a stoplight, a taillight...*

Using post-hypnotict suggestion to tye everyday experiences to success is a powerful way to generate more success.

AWAKENING
Orientation to Surroundings
Energize
Direct Suggestion to Open Eyes

The awakening process is an important part of the script, because it helps my client become comfortable, alert, and aware while returning to the present moment in the conscious mind.

Awakening scripts are generally pretty simple. I personally think people should be awakened in a nice and polite way. I almost always do a number count-up, after reinforcing the learning process. Here's an example:

> *You've done a great job learning new skills and creating your own state of creativity and intuition. It is now time, though, to reorient to the room around you.*
>
> *And so, even though your eyes can remain closed for a moment, you can still feel the chair below you, and the floor below your feet, and as you become more aware of the room around you can continue to enjoy the state of hypnosis that you've created.*
>
> *And as I count up from one to five, with each number allow yourself to become more alert, more refreshed, returning to a state of awareness.*
>
> *One, becoming more alert.*

Two, moving the neck and stretching out any muscles that need to be stretched.

Three, feeling more alert, taking in a deep breath.

Four, opening the eyes, wide open, feeling wonderful.

And, five, totally awake, totally alert, totally refreshed.

AFTER THE SESSION
Check for Time Distortion—Proof
Review Suggestions
Reschedule Appointment

Check for Time Distortion—Proof

After I do a session, I want my clients to know that they were hypnotized. At the end, if I can ratify that something happened during this process, they leave believing something happened, and take action on this—i.e. making the changes they came to me for help with.

Earlier you learned that I use trance ratification suggestions to take my clients deeper into hypnosis, and I also use a similar strategy immediately after the session is over.

My friend and colleague John Cerbone uses what he calls a "proof," where he gives the client a suggestion that they will wake up and find the color red to be funny—specifically, his red pen. He tells them that when they open their eyes they will laugh at the red pen he is holding.

This technique works very well, but I never have red pens handy. Instead, I use the phenomena of time distortion as a proof or ratification of the process.

Immediately after the session is over, I ask the client:

How long did that session feel?

I time every session, so I always know the answer, and usually my sessions are about 35 minutes. Here are the answers I commonly get, and my patter for each reply:

80% of the people look confused by the question (that is good), and think for a moment before saying about 5-10 minutes. I then use this patter:

> *Awesome! This is called time distortion. When a person is hypnotized they often experience confusion about time. In reality our session was almost 35 minutes, so your time distortion was off by 400%. That means you did a great job and will have no trouble acting on the suggestions in our session. Congratulations!*

15% of the time the client says something like, "Well I know it could not have been 2 hours (or 2 days), but it sure felt like it!" In this situation, time distortion is reversed, and here is what I say:

> *Awesome! This is called time distortion. Often when a person is hypnotized time speeds up or slows down. For you it seemed to really slow down. Perhaps this is the unconscious mind really processing information and new learnings. That means you have really been able to take these suggestions to heart and will do great. Congratulations!*

About 5% of of the time a client looks at me and says, "Oh, I don't know, about 35 minutes?"

This does not mean that they were not hypnotized, it just means they did not experience the natural phenomena of time distortion—which is fine, because I never suggested that they would, it just sometimes happens on its own—and so my reply to this is:

> Great! You are right, it was about 35 minutes. That means you payed attention the whole time and never got lost in your thoughts, able to always focus on the suggestions. I know that you will do great, so congratulations!

Review Suggestions

After every session I take a few minutes and process with clients the suggestions I gave. For some reason other hypnotists do not do this. I think it serves two purposes.

First, it gives me a few more minutes with them in the chair, and this time is also used by me to make sure they are fully alert, stable, and oriented before I put them in a car to drive home.

Second, it brings to the conscious mind that which has been learned or processed in the subconscious mind. There is no reason not to tell clients what suggestions you have gave. After all, that is what they paid you for, and the suggestions are in fact "property" of the client, in my opinion.

And so I ask my clients,

> Do you remember some of the suggestions I gave you?

I give them time to answer. If the client cannot easily recall the suggestions, I say this:

> Not being able to recall the many suggestions I gave you shows you were in deep trance, and that is good. Here are some of the suggestions I gave you.

Do you recall these: (I then list three or four of the major suggestions).

If the client does remember the suggestions, they will start articulating them. Here is my reply after they come up with three or four of them:

Perfect, I am glad that you were able to really pay attention and internalize those suggestions. That tells me you are able to start taking action on them now. You will do very well!

Schedule the Next Appointment

I find scheduling a session immediately following the current session is the best way to make certain clients follow through and set the next session. I say this:

Before you go, let's look at the schedule and set our next meeting. I am free next _____ or _____ in the (mornings, afternoons). Does either of those times work for you, or is there a better time?

A NOTE ABOUT PRACTICE

These are all simple structures of patter for effective suggestions, and I hope they have been valuable to you. In the next section we'll discuss more elements of effective patter, but the above is the general structure you will want to use.

All of these phases of the hypnosis session can and should be planned ahead of time, whether they are written down word-for-word, outlined, or planned internally.

The more scripts you write out, the more comfortable you will become creating them on the fly with new clients, and with the language or patter in general.

Practice the phrasing—write it down, read it out loud, commit it to memory.

Set aside an hour every weekend, or any time you have free time during the week, and write down lists of good direct suggestions for various common client concerns. These may be complete paragraphs, one sentence, or a general concept. Write down enough for you to explore and be comfortable with the phrasing and delivery of the suggestion.

Do this exercise for smoking cessation, weight loss, anxiety, specific phobias, confidence building, sports performance, pain management, and so forth, again and again. This will build your confidence and skills.

This is also building your very own script book resource, that you will use more than you could imagine over the coming years.

Richard K. Nongard

KEY ELEMENTS FOR EFFECTIVE PATTER AND SCRIPT BUILDING

In the previous section we discussed the structure of a session, from when the client enters the office, through induction, suggestive therapy, and awakening. Now, I want to discuss some key concepts of language structure and style that will further increase the efficacy of your patter and script-writing skills.

Positive Suggestions

The first key concept, which we discussed briefly but warrants more emphasis, is that the suggestive language you use —whether during pre-talk convincers, the induction, or during suggestive therapy—needs to be positive.

Positive suggestions are received by the subconscious mind ten times more easily than negative suggestions. Think about this: During our whole life, we've been primed to resist negative suggestions. Don't sneak out of work early. Don't speed in your automobile. Don't talk back to your mother. Most of the suggestions we hear come in the form of rules and negative suggestions, and we say, "Yeah, yeah yeah, I know I know," and then we proceed to speed and sneak out, and even talk back now and then, even though we know the consequences.

Effective suggestions need to be phrased in a positive way. Even if a client comes to us to quit using cigarettes, pot, or even cocaine, our viewpoint should be not that they they are quitting something that they liked doing, but that they are starting to do something different that they like even more (breathing clean air, being healthy, removing legal consequences, and so forth).

For example, I had a client years ago who was referred to me for therapy by his father. I didn't actually know his father personally, but his dad was also a therapist and attended one of my continuing education seminars, and I guess he liked what I had to say. His son was a pot smoker and had a lot of other things going on as well, and the father had sent him to many different treatment programs with no success, so now he was sending the son to me.

So, in the first session, the 19-year-old kid says to me, "Well, you're not going to tell me to quit smoking pot like all my dad's other shrink friends are, are you?"

To which I replied, "One, I've only met your dad once, so I'm not really your dad's friend, but, two, no, I'm not going to tell you to quit smoking pot like everyone else has."

He said, "Really? Are you a pot smoker?"

I said, "No, no, no, I'm not a pot smoker. But I'm smart enough to know that if I tell you to quit smoking pot like your dad's other friends have, you won't listen to me. So instead, I'm going to help you learn how to love life so much that you won't want to miss any of it by being drunk or high or stoned."

He was skeptical, but he listened, and he saw that I was right. The key was positive reframing and positive suggestion.

My clients don't give up their morning cigarettes. Instead, they learn how to derive energy by breathing in a deep cleansing breath and feeling the oxygen spread to every cell in their body.

My client doesn't give up chocolate cake. Instead, they learn how to eat enough food to satisfy their nutritional needs and to feel their hunger is quenched, and then simply move on to whatever it is that they need to do next—dishes, walking, game night.

Positive suggestions are extremely important:

Instead of decreasing our pain, let's increase our comfort.

Clear Concepts

Any metaphors, stories, or parables we use have to be easily understood by the individual client.

I meet hypnotherapists all the time who come up with all kinds of nifty, interesting metaphors and stories—that really are very difficult for the average person to understand. Sometimes they get them from heavy literature, at a hypnosis seminar, and that's all fine and good, but quite often these anecdotes are not really related to the person sitting in front of us.

Stories, metaphors, and parables that we use should not need to be explained to the client; they should be easy for them to grasp either literally or conceptually, especially in our first or second hypnosis session.

As we spend more time with the client and come to understand them more individually, our metaphors, stories, and parables can perhaps become deeper, but we should base that decision on knowing that our client can understand the concepts given with both the conscious and the subconscious mind.

Specific Topics

Effective suggestions stick to a specific topic. If a person comes to me for smoking sensation, I don't try to also get them to quit eating Twinkies, be nice to their mother, or stop chasing cars. All I have them do is become smoke-free. If a client comes in for weight loss, I don't also help them build their confidence in public speaking situations, overcome their fear of flying, and manage their back pain.

Now, it may be true sometimes that one issue they discuss is related to another, but at least in the first session we stick to the initial or primary topic, and then perhaps in the second or third we will combine and address the related issues for enhanced success.

For example, cigarette smokers are often afraid that they will gain weight if they quit smoking. Therefore, one of the things I teach my smokers during the pre-talk is that the reason the ex-smoker gains weight is because nicotine is a drug that affects their metabolism, and if they quit smoking, their metabolic change results in 100 to 200 calories less per day being burned. So all they need to do is increase their activity level 100 to 200 calories per day. This subject is weight and exercise, but it is directly related to smoking cessation, and if they are concerned enough, it may actually impact their smoke-free success.

So, in my suggestions I may very well say:

Increase your activity each day by taking more steps today than yesterday, and more steps tomorrow than today, increasing your activity level each and every day from this point forward.

This great suggestion is an easy way to help people increase their activity level, simply by walking a little bit more each and every day.

I avoid doing combination sessions where the goal is to produce a super person all at once—cure a phobia, lose weight, and get over a lost love—because suggestions are more effectively responded to when they are of a single purpose.

Present Tense

When possible, keep the concepts and suggestive language used in the present tense. It's not necessarily only in the future that the client will do these things, but *now* that they are doing these things.

For example: They are not *going to become a non-smoker,* because they have *already become a non-smoker.*

How do I know that? Because they came to this session today and asked me to help them become a non-smoker. I'm not going to talk about their future success as a non-smoker; during the hypnotherapy session I'm going to address them from the present tense perspective of having already succeeded at the goal that already brought them to my office.

Utilize Existing Strengths and Resources

Draw on the client's strengths that pre-exit. For example, is my client trustworthy, friendly, loyal, courteous, kind, obedient, cheerful, thrifty, brave, clean, reverent? Yes, they came in because they have some negative issue that they want to address or change, but what is *right* with my client? What internal strengths—personality attributes and characteristics—do they possess that have helped them be successful in other areas to this point?

Those strengths are things that I want to draw upon in my scripting.

> *You are always loyal to your friends and family, and you are loyal to yourself, making healthy positive choices that are true to your needs and desires.*

Resources are the practical things that my client has available to them. Rather than me trying to find or give them new resources, why not have them draw on the resources that already exist?

For example, let's say a client wants to quit using drugs. Hypnosis helps them quit, but they desire to make new 'clean' friends, and they want to attend Narcotics Anonymous meetings. Well, do they have a car? Do they have a telephone? Do they have any specific people in their world (neighbor, mother, pastor, coworker) willing to support their goals? Those are resources.

And so, what I want to do with my clients is help them identify their existing strengths and resources that can help them solve a particular dilemma, and then my suggestions are going to be based on these things that are already present.

Utilizing the client's resources is so important and valuable that we put together a strength and resources assessment tool, which I've taught to hundreds of therapists over the years. If you're interested in understanding how to use strengths and resources in hypnotherapy, I highly recommend you use the NSRI **"Nongard Strengths and Resources Inventory"** as a tool for helping assess client assets and monitor their progress. You can find a copy of it in Appendix A.

Realistic, Practical, and Healthy

The suggestions we give need to be healthy and actually attainable. Some folks will come in to the office with either unhealthy or unrealistic expectations. For example, they may come in and say, "Gosh, my daughter's wedding is next month, and I need to loose 30 pounds—a pound a day. Hypnosis can do that, right?"

They perceive this goal as somehow being realistic, and while technically it may be possible, it certainly isn't healthy. A realistic and healthy weight loss goal is anywhere from two to five pounds the first week, and one-and-a-half to three-and-a-half, depending on their size and whether they are a man or woman, each following week. Using this math, healthy weight loss over the next four weeks is going to be about ten pounds. That's a goal that is obtainable and healthy.

I do not want to assist my clients with either unrealistic or unhealthy goals. It's okay for a person to set their sights high. I'm not going to discount their vision for success, but I may have to help them redefine their goals so that they're not unhealthy.

For example, I don't want to help a client feel no pain. Pain is an indicator that change needs to take place. Pain protects a person; it lets us know what our limits are. So I would never work with a pain client to completely eliminate pain, but instead to help them increase their comfort level and understand what their pain is trying to tell them.

Engage All Senses

Take a sensory approach. In elementary school, we learned that there are five senses: sight, sound, touch, taste, smell.

We interpret the world around us from a sensory perspective. The way we learn and perceive our surroundings comes from a sensory understanding: audio, visual, and kinesthetic.

In my suggestion scripting, I want to increase my client's sensory awareness of change and success.

I am a licensed marriage and family therapist, and therefore I work with couples in regards to sexual difficulties. One assignment I often use is to give them a piece of paper, a pen and about ten minutes, and instruct them to, as a team, write down lists of adjectives that describe sex, from each of the five sensory perspectives: the sight of sex, the sound of sex, the touch of sex, the smell of sex, the taste of sex.

Now depending on their situation they might feel a little awkward or silly at first, but usually they lighten up pretty quickly and have fun with the assignment. And in the end, they emerge with an entirely new perspective on sex and sexual experiences.

Incorporating the five senses into our suggestive therapy is extremely effective. The sound of success (sports performance), inhaling and exhaling clean smelling air (quitting smoking), the taste of fresh vegetables (weight loss), the feel of walking upright with confidence (self-esteem), the vision of graduation day (test-taking anxiety), and so forth.

Individualized, Customized Suggestions

Every client is different, and has different goals and needs. Your therapeutic suggestions should always be tailored to the individual client.

Go ahead and write down metaphorical stories and parables you have discovered somewhere (or that you make up) that are related to the clients you are working with. And, you should also write down specific direct suggestions—but to be most effective, these have to come directly or indirectly from the client themselves.

Ask you clients: What is your goal? What is it that you want to accomplish by being here? Their answers will tell you what they want you to suggest to them. So, when you write out your script—or jot down notes—write down what they want.

All therapists have their own individual styles and approaches, and personally, I never do aversion therapy because, as we discussed, positive suggestions are far more effective than negative suggestions. Well, I shouldn't say never; if I use it, it's for a very specific reason.

For example, I had a seventy-year-old lady come in to quit smoking and say, "I want you to know that I've been to a hypnotherapist before, and it didn't work. And I've tried to quit smoking by doing this, this, this, and this..." She said the only reason she was here was to make her son happy, and as a matter of fact, he paid for the session.

Now, had she not continued on with what she said next, I probably wouldn't have done the session with her, because I think that people need to be not only personally motivated, but also invested in their own treatment, as well as having a realistic belief that hypnosis will help them reach their goal. Otherwise, what's the point?

But she said all these negative things, and then she said, "I suppose there's really only one way I could quit smoking..." (By the way, she just used the embedded command to herself, "I could quit smoking"). She said, "I could quit smoking if you were to suggest to me that I would puke, that I would become sick, that I wouldn't even like a cigarette anymore."

As I said, normally I don't do aversion therapy, but she told me specifically what she wanted me to suggest to her, and she also had already given herself the suggestion, "I could quit smoking."

So I swooped her right into the office and did an aversion therapy session, even though it's not an approach that I traditionally feel comfortable using. When she left my office I wondered if she would do well or not, but four months later I heard back from her son and she had continued to be a non-smoker, for the very first time in 56 years.

And so, suggestions have to be individualized. If we ask questions and listen and take notes, our clients will tell us what it is (the magic words) that we're supposed to suggest to them.

Utilize Dominant Emotions

Use what many call the Law of Dominant Effect. This law means that a stronger emotion will replace a weaker emotion. To make this concept functional in hypnosis, we have to attach significant, powerful emotion to our suggestions.

When you derive energy from oxygen rather than from nicotine, you feel —- ?

Significant emotions are the key for effectiveness.

Which sounds more powerful:

You feel good.

Good. Well, good is okay. It's positive, and it's generally thought to be better than bad.

You feel better.

Better. Better than what? Better than ever? Well, how much better? A little better or a lot better? Better is a loose term that should generally be avoided, because it's rather open ended—it's not significant.

You feel great.

Great. Great is pretty awesome, isn't it? It's rather undefinable, like better, but it is a step or three above.

How about this statement instead:

When you derive energy from oxygen rather than from nicotine, you feel happy about this, excited. You feel a sense of pride and success.

Everyone wants to be *happy*, even if that is also a rather loose term. We all have an idea in our head on what happy should be like, and that's what we all always strive for—to be happy.

Excited. Wow, when is the last time that most of us were excited about anything? Being excited is a big deal, because it's a little more rare, and it's a significant emotion.

Pride. We all want to feel proud, but many people don't feel they have much in the way of accomplishments or situations to be proud of in their every day life. Feeling proud is significant.

Success. Success is huge. Success is something to be proud of, as it means you have done something worthy of praise. Success is very significant.

As you write scripts and develop patter for suggestive therapy, remember to attach significant positive emotion to the suggestions.

You feel not only empowered to be able to make these healthy choices at a buffet, but also excited about the new opportunities you have to see eating from a new perspective.

These are magic words.

Richard K. Nongard

SUGGESTIVE PATTER: PHRASES, CONCEPTS, AND ANSWERS

This section contains dozens of helpful patter phrases or script snippets designed to help you know what to say and/or do when various situations arise in your clinical office.

Can you use this patter word for word? Sure, I suppose. These are the things I say when faced with these challenges or questions, and these words work for me.

My intention, however, is not to have you copy me directly, but to see what you could do—to get the basic idea—and then modify the language or phrasing to fit your own personal delivery style and therapeutic approach. Over time, you will develop your own brilliant patter, and with it, the ability to handle any situation that might arise.

When Meeting a New Client who has Never been Hypnotized

When I first meet someone who has never been hypnotized, I want to give my first suggestion, even before I formally hypnotize them. Confidence in yourself, and instilling confidence in the client, are really the keys to the rest of the session. Deliver these lines with confidence, matter-of-factly, and set this up as essentially the first suggestion.

Have you ever experienced hypnosis before?

No.

Great, I love working with people who are learning a new skill—you will do very well...

When Meeting a New Client who has been Previously Hypnotized by Someone Else

I am surprised at how many people make an appointment in my office, even though they have had a less than professional experience in another office. But, people often still understand that hypnosis is a useful tool, even though another hypnotist they tried was ineffective.

Of course, there are others who did have positive experiences, and perhaps moved or for some reason must find a new hypnotist, and this should be dealt with also. Here is my patter for both situations.

Was it helpful?

Answer 1: Yes

Awesome! I know you will find this session, although different, very valuable also, perhaps even in some new ways.

Answer 2: No

I am glad you came here though. Different hypnotists have different strategies. During this initial interview I will be determining what the best strategies for you will be, and when I can match my techniques and suggestions to your learning style, hypnosis is very effective. One tool I use to help with this is the Nongard Assessment of Primary Representational Systems, it can help me identify your primary learning style so I can match it. This simple technique, matching my session style to your learning style can make all the difference....

When the Client is Anxious

Although people who are truly fearful of hypnosis usually do not make an appointment with a hypnotist, going to see a hypnotist is a new experience, and general anxiety about new experiences is normal. This does not mean they do not want to be hypnotized; it simply means they feel anxiety about new experiences. They probably felt this way the first time they went to a new class, or even on the first day of a job. It is not a sign of resistance, but rather a normal human response to the unknown.

Here is the patter I use to calm a new client:

Other people have been anxious when they first came to a session, and then they find hypnosis is very relaxing. I am actually going to teach you how to calm anxiety during our session, so you will do fine.

Of course if at any time you are uncomfortable during our session, you can let me know. It's okay to open your eyes or even ask me a question, and we can easily deal with any remaining anxiety before it disappears.

When a Client has Doubts

Truly skeptical clients rarely make an appointment for hypnosis; they tend to prefer medication or staying stuck. But there are clients who, despite their desire to change using hypnosis, are skeptical of its ability to really help them. They simply do not understand how you are going to help them.

The following explanation seems to make sense to most of my clients who have a degree of skepticism.

> *I am like a coach. You have inside of you a desire for change or you would not have made the appointment today, and so my job is to help you bring that desire to the point of success. I have helped many people do this, and so if you really want to make a change, together we can cross the finish line, as remarkable as that seems.*

Richard K. Nongard

Words that Normalize Hypnosis

Psychologists in the 1960s began describing hypnosis as an "altered state" of consciousness, even though hypnosis is natural phenomena that each of us naturally experiences every day. Unfortunately, this description has self-replicated over the years, and the definition of "altered-state" became even more strange and twisted with the Hollywood blockbuster release in 1980 of a film called "Altered States." And so when clients come into our office, they often want hypnosis but have misconceptions, believing hypnosis to be what psychologists have told them, an altered state, and they assume it will feel just like Hollywood has portrayed that altered state.

Here is what I say to normalize hypnosis:

Hypnosis is a natural state. It exists in our everyday lives. When you drive while talking on the phone, you subconscious is driving the car. When you laugh or cry at a movie, you know it's not real, but the creative part of your mind is able to respond with the appropriate emotion.

Hypnosis is just like everyday life, in that all of the experience you will have are experiences you have already had in life; we are just directing these creative energies to learning new things and establishing new patterns of behavior

Magic Words

Words that Define Hypnosis for Clients

Hypnosis comes from the root Greek word for sleep, and stage hypnotists have been shouting "Sleeeep!" for over a century, and so clients often do not know what hypnosis is, and many think they will be sleeping or somehow unconscious.

This is what I tell new clients so they will understand what hypnosis is in my office:

> *Hypnosis is not sleep, even though you have heard the word "sleep" associated with hypnosis. Nor is it unconsciousness.*
>
> *You will always be able to hear my voice; you will always know where you are.*
>
> *Hypnosis is really a state of creative enhancement and openness to new learnings, much like a state of focused concentration.*

To Help Clients Feel Safe

Clients need to feel safe—safe emotionally, safe from outside intrusion, and even safe from the hypnotist.

This language generally helps people who may have safety or security issues to feel more comfortable:

> *I have worked with many people, right here and in this room. Always safe, always relaxed, knowing that this is where you will begin to make remarkable changes.*
>
> *You are always in control, always able to speak, and even able to open your eyes.*
>
> *Perfectly safe, with me over here speaking into my microphone, and you in the chair hearing my words.*

To Let Clients Know they are in Control

Letting clients know they are actually in control shifts the responsibility for change to the client, and also promotes a sense of safety and comfort.

Of course, you know that you always control the process of hypnosis.

You can choose to accept or reject these ideas, or even open or close your eyes.

But you have come here today to make changes, and so the suggestions I am giving you are actually suggestions that you have asked me to make today.

It is you who is the operator of this session, almost really a relationship where I am following your lead, and you are taking me with you on your journey of success.

To Establish your Role

By establishing my role, and clearly assigning responsibility to clients rather than the mystical process of hypnosis, I find greater levels of success.

Here is what I tell clients:

I am much like a teacher or a coach.

Although I cannot take the action for you, I know what works to (solve X problem) and have worked with many others guiding them to positive solutions.

I will also be guiding you, in part from my experience working with others, and in part based on the suggestions you have asked me to make by coming here today.

Words to Reverse Role

Reversing roles was a favorite technique of Milton Erickson. This process assigns responsibility for change to the clients, and is an element of confusion, which can be useful in induction.

It is amazing how hypnosis really works. It is as if I am following you, and you are leading me.

In fact, you do all of the work making these changes, and I get to sit in my chair simply watching your success germinate.

To Get Paid

Asking for payment is always a source of frustration to people who provide services. Part of us wants to be paid up front, since a service cannot be returned, and part of us (the consumer side) wants the client to pay afterwards so they will not be uneasy.

Personally, I collect payment before I ever do any session. When they first come in the office, I use the following statement when I give them the initial intake and assessment forms to complete:

> *When you called we discussed the fee of $259 for this session. As you fill out these forms, I will get your receipt.*
>
> *Are you going to be paying with a check, cash or a credit card?*
>
> (wait for answer)
>
> *Okay, I will process that now while you're completing the paperwork.*

When a Client is Not Prepared to Pay Today

I tell all clients two things on both the phone and my website: First, session payments are expected at the first session. Second, I do not file nor accept insurance as payment.

Occasionally though, a client is still not prepared to make payment when they arrive for the first session.

Here is how I handle that situation in both first sessions with a new client, and in successive sessions with an established client.

First Session: (if they truly forgot in this first session)

> *We keep our fees reasonably priced by requiring prepay, but I understand you have forgotten your checkbook, cash, or credit card. You can use our computer to send payment via PayPal, where you can use a credit or debit card.*

Or—

> *We are happy to help you, and will email you an invoice today. Invoices are due within seven days, but you can pay it online for your convenience using PayPal with your credit or debit card.*

Second session:

> *I can send you an invoice via PayPal and you can pay it today. Invoices are due within 7 days, or before your next scheduled session.*

In a third or later session, or if it becomes a pattern, it is a serious sign of resistance to the therapeutic progress. I will give them one chance:

> *Do you have a PayPal account? I will let you use my computer to make a transfer.*
>
> *Fees are due when services are provided. We can continue with this session as long as we can agree that when you return home this evening you will send the money via my website or PayPal with your credit card.*

When Questioned about High Fees

Rarely do clients ask if my fees are "worth it" or why they are so high. My fees are posted on my website, and I make a point to inform them on the phone before they come to the first session. They would not be booking a session if they thought they were too high.

But on occasion, I have used the following statement to help them understand the cash value of my services:

My fees are consistent with other professionals who produce excellent results. And although they are perhaps more expensive than a plumber's house call fee, the good news is they are less than a lawyer or accountant.

(Or to emphasis the point with the right client, an oncology physician.)

Do you have a Guarantee?

Many hypnosis CDs are promoted with a "money-back" guarantee, and even a few hypnotists have touted guarantees of one type or another.

Like most hypnotists though, I do not offer a guarantee. There is no way for me to truly guarantee anything, since client success is more dependent on them and their follow-through than on me or even my skill level. I am uninterested in the "cheesiness" or the occasional hassle a guarantee would cause, so when asked if I have a guarantee, here is my response:

> I do! I guarantee that I will provide my time to help you with competent and professional services.
>
> I can also guarantee that if you follow the suggestions I offer, you will experience the desired outcome. Most of my clients do.
>
> What I cannot guarantee is that you will not be one of the few clients who fails to follow my suggestions when you leave the office, does not listen to the CD I provide, and does not follow through on recommendations.
>
> Your success is as dependent on you as it is me, and so no, there is not a money-back guarantee, just like there is not one in any medical or psychological clinic where success is often dependent on the client as much as it is the provider.

When there is Background Noise

Sometimes background noise from other offices, cars and even unexpected construction will be clearly heard during a session. I use a sound system in my office, and clients wear headphones to hear both my voice and music. This minimizes outside distractions, but they do still happen.

The answer is to simply make it part of the session, giving them the suggestion that this will not bother them, and will actually help them.

> *You might hear the sounds of cars honking outside in the parking lot, or workers in the building, or even the mail man coming in to deliver mail. These things will not disturb you, in fact they will reassure you that you are exactly where you need to be, doing exactly what you need to be doing that is best for you, and reassures you and help you to relax.*

Or simply—

> *Any background noise you hear will not disturb you; in fact it helps you to feel even more comfortable, recognizing you are exactly where you need to be and doing exactly what you need to be doing.*

How to Prepare for Potential Interruptions

Even in a well planned hypnosis center, there can be interruptions. People poke heads into the wrong office, mailmen seem to always come in for a signature during a session, and phones may unexpectedly ring. If you are careful and clever, no matter the daily or surprise background noise, you can set up suggestions during the induction process so that any potential interruptions simply become part of the hypnosis session.

If there are any interruptions in our session, you will be able to continue to relax and remain hypnotized, recognizing that if the postman comes in, or if a phone rings, or even if something outside of this office demands your attention, you have the ability to direct your attention to that which is necessary, and remain relaxed and open to new learnings.

What if a Cell Phone Rings During the Session

I usually do not bring my cell phone into the office where I do sessions, and during the intake time I ask clients to turn off their phone.

That being said, there are still times a phone will ring, and so here is what I say, even throwing in a little post-hypnotic positive suggestion:

Do not worry about the phone disturbing you. Sometimes people accidentally leave them on.

If you need to, you can open your eyes and turn off the ringer, but if you are comfortable just let it ring, and when the ringing stops let yourself go into an even deeper trance.

In fact, in everyday life we hear the phone many times a day and from this point forward, let it be a reminder to you of the progress or decision you have made, and let it bring a smile to your face as you recall this moment of change that you create here today.

When Time is Short

Just the other day, I had a noon appointment and a 1:30 pm appointment. This would have been fine, except the noon appointment showed up at 12:30 pm. When clients are late I do not extend their time, but rather do a shorter session.

Here are the magic words to bring someone into trance quickly, if they have experienced hypnosis before:

Many people worry about being able to do hypnosis quickly, but in stage hypnosis it is done all the time.

You know what that state of learning and relaxation feels like, so close your eyes now and bring yourself to that frame or state....

Are you there?

Perfect, now I am going to give you suggestions, you can act instantly upon, internalizing them and confidently following, even long after this brief session is over...

When a Client is Sleepy

Sometimes clients come to a session sleepy, and this can be a challenge at times, as we do not want them nodding off once they are relaxed.

> *Sleepy is good, as it will be easy for you to relax, but I want to make sure you do not fall asleep instead of experiencing hypnosis, so today we are going to do this session in the banquet chair rather than the recliner.*

Or

> *Don't worry about falling asleep. I will be asking you to do certain things in this session and asking for feedback along the way, so you can let yourself relax, but know you can pay attention to every word and suggestion I give, never asleep, but deeply relaxed.*

To Avoid Clients Falling Asleep

Clients do not usually fall asleep. But if they seem to be heading that way, the direct suggestion to stay awake or engage the conscious mind works.

As you relax, you might find it would be easy to just go to sleep, but even in a very relaxed state your mind always open to new ideas and creativity.

And so as you relax, never asleep, you know your mind continues to remain awake, even as you feel physically relaxed and still.

And anytime you find yourself drifting over that line of relaxation and into sleep, just bring your attention back to my words and the room around you, remaining focused on your new learnings.

When a Client is Emotional

Emotions are normal, and every hypnotist's office should have a box of Kleenex tissues handy. Clients will cry on occasion, and this is normal—it is not "abreaction."

It is okay to have strong emotions. That is why I always keep these boxes of Kleenex in my office. This is the right place, and a safe place to feel _____. So just take a breath and know you are in the right place.

Or:

Tears are normal. Sometime tears of sadness or even hope come during sessions. That is perfectly normal and why I have Kleenex in my office. You can take all the time you need to feel _____. Feelings let us know we are a human being, not a human doing—and that is a good thing.

When a Client is Unfocused

Clients may come into the office unfocused. They have many tasks in life, ranging from remembering when to pick up their children to endless cell phone calls to responsibilities at work. Scheduling one more thing, a hypnosis session in the middle of the day, may result in clients coming into the office unfocused, and at the beginning of the induction you will be able to sense this.

You seem a bit distracted today. Distraction is okay; it shows you are really looking for something. What is it you would like to find?

Or

Now pick a point on the far wall, and notice how you can bring all of your attention and energy to it. In fact it is as if all distractions have been pushed aside... and so anytime you find yourself distracted, bring your attention back to that point on the wall. You can even do this when your eyes are closed by imagining that point.

When a Client's Mind is Wandering

During the induction, especially the very first few moments, a wandering mind may concern a client. I have had many people say it was at first hard for them to be hypnotized because they were not sure if it was okay that their mind kept wondering.

I use this patter to "normalize" a wandering mind:

As you relax, you might even notice your mind wandering or becoming distracted. That is okay, after all this is what minds do—they wander. When you notice this, gently return your focus to what is important, and in a few minutes we will focus on an exercise to still the mind.

(I then move towards creative visualization exercises.)

When Clients Say they are More Comfortable in an Odd Position

Our job is to work with clients as they come to us, rather than the way we wish they were. No one wins a power struggle. If my indirect suggestion does not produce a change in posture, I just go with it, letting them control the way they sit. Pick your battles wisely. This is not one I mind loosing, although I prefer a more traditional posture.

> *If it's more comfortable to continue to be in that position, that is fine; it is up to you to create the experience that is most helpful to you, but if at a later time you need to shift for comfort or would find it easier in a different position, please feel free to adjust for your benefit.*

To Put Clients into Hypnotic Posture

The best posture for hypnosis in my opinion is either relaxing in a recliner with the footrest extended, or sitting in a banquet type chair with upright posture—a straight spine and the head tilted forward.

In my office I have comfortable recliners. I tell clients to kick back in the recliner using the lever to create a footrest. They almost always then cross their arm or legs out of habit, and so I ask them to uncross.

If clients are not instructed to uncross the arms and legs, this can become uncomfortable as the weight pressure can cause loss of circulation and the feeling that their "legs are falling asleep," which can be distracting, and even dangerous when they go to stand later. Furthermore, uncrossing their arms is important because I often set anchors with the hands, and I also want to create various sensations of warmth and heaviness that are experienced better if the hands are to the side or on the lap.

The phrase "letting your chin drop towards your chest" is not used when they are in a recliner, for obvious reasons. I only use this if they are sitting in a chair or on my small loveseat. In a recliner, the head is automatically tiled back on the headrest.

I use these postures because they are comfortable, yet allow for deep breathing. The chair position also keeps people form falling asleep, a risk that is slightly increased in the recliner. Interestingly, beginning meditation classes also encourage the use of a chair, and the exact same posture.

I use this as part of my initial induction to direct clients into a hypnotic posture:

> *The posture for hypnosis is important. Please uncross your legs and arms, letting yourself relax comfortably with your hands to the side or resting on the chair.*
>
> *You can also move your buttocks back into the chair so you don't feel like you are sliding. Perfect.*
>
> *And finally, relax your neck and shoulders, letting your chin drop towards your chest. Relaxed and unrestricted, ready to go easily into a state of hypnosis.*

What if a Client's Legs or Arms are Crossed

As mentioned above, I generally do not like when clients restrict blood flow and comfort by remaining with their legs crossed or arms folded, especially if they are new to hypnosis, but sometimes during a session when they "adjust for comfort" they will re-cross their arms or legs, out of habit.

Here is an indirect way to get them to sit in a better posture for hypnosis:

Many people find it easier to be comfortable if they uncross the arms and legs. During our session I may ask you to use your hands to create a signal or create an anchor, and it will be easier if your hands are resting comfortably on your lap or to the side.

When Clients Do Not Close their Eyes

If clients do not close their eyes during hypnosis, it usually means they feel unsafe, or are resistant for some reason.

I do not mind doing a session with the eyes open; hypnosis is done with the eyes open in stage hypnosis all the time, so I have no problem giving clients this option in clinical hypnosis. However, most of the time they will eventually decide to close them.

> Most people find closing the eyes is more comfortable. But others find keeping the eyes open is more comfortable. Would you like to do this session with your eyes open, or with your eyes closed?

Closed:

> Then close your eyes now, letting your eyelids become heavy and relaxed. You know of course you could open them if you wanted to, but you will find it is easier to just keep them closed.

Open:

> Great. One does not have to close the eyes to experience hypnosis, but if at any time you find that it would be more comfortable to close the eyes you can let them close, and stay closed.

Until then, pick a point on the far wall (or anywhere) and just direct your attention and awareness to that spot, keeping your eyes open but following my suggestions to.....

When Clients Do Not Follow Initial Suggestions in Preparation and Induction

Rarely do resistant clients actually make an appointment with a hypnotist. If they do, it is usually because a family member pressured them to come. So occasionally we will have to deal with someone who does not follow initial suggestions for induction, despite a good pre-talk.

Here is what I say to them:

I have given you several suggestions, (for example), to take a deep breath, to close your eyes, and to uncross your arms.

You have not followed these suggestions.

I am concerned that if you are not following these simple suggestions now, when we get to the suggestions related to what you want to accomplish, you will not follow those.

So tell me, what do you need to do or know to follow the suggestions I have already given you?

When Clients Laugh During Induction

Newer hypnotists often wonder, "What if someone starts laughing?" I actually don't mind this, as it is easy to use laughter as a healing modality.

Sure the laughter may come from embarrassment or skepticism, but even in these cases it can be utilized as part of any induction. Stage hypnotists are experts in dealing with laughing subjects.

This is the line I use in my stage hypnosis shows, and it works just as well in clinical hypnosis:

> *It is perfectly okay to laugh a bit or even giggle. Laughter is the best medicine, as a matter of fact, so when you laugh or smile it is good for you, helping you to relax even further.*

You can also utilize opposition by acknowledging the obvious:

> *Sure it's funny to come to an office and be hypnotized. It is not something we normally do in life. The conscious mind might even find it silly, but that is okay, because as you laugh, you can turn that into a real joy over your ability to really make change.*

What if a Client says, "I Just Can't Do This"

Every now and then a client is so overwhelmed by making change and by following directions they just give up. Although this does not happen often, it is really a cry for help and more specific direction, rather than truly giving up. They also need perhaps, a little more pre-talk to help them understand that they do not have to try to be hypnotized, it is natural.

Go ahead and open the eyes. Take a breath.

Are you having a hard time with experiencing hypnosis, or are you not ready to address these issues?

If they're having a hard time with hypnosis:

One does not even have to be hypnotized to benefit from the process. You can do this. There is no special state required, and you came here today to be successful, so stop trying to be hypnotized.

It's kind of like at night when you try to sleep it becomes difficult, and so just follow the process whether you are hypnotized or not.

Follow up with:

You may even be wondering now is this what it is like to be hypnotized, or perhaps you have noticed by simply following the process you have entered that creative state of hypnosis. Either way is fine, just continue to follow the process because it is a learning process, and you are doing great.

If they say they are not ready:

It is a great ability to recognize your own opposition to change. It often means one wants the benefits of (insert negative behavior here) *but without the consequences.*

During our session I am going to give you suggestions for motivation, but more importantly, to help you keep those things that are important or meaningful to you but with new behaviors.

What if Clients Say they Aren't Hypnotized

This situation is different than the client who says, "I can't be hypnotized." This refers to the person who becomes frustrated, opens their eyes and says, "I am not hypnotized!"

Note to hypnotists: You must deal with this issue in this session, but please recognize that this problem could likely have been avoided by utilizing convincers and clear explanation during the pre-talk, and assessing for positive reactions.

If this happens, say:

Hypnosis is a process, not something I am doing to you. You will either feel hypnotized or not, as your mind chooses to feel hypnosis, but either way you will able to use the suggestions I give to make change, regardless of the feeling.

One thing you can do is just imagine you are hypnotized, even though you know you are not, and continue with the process. The benefits are the same.

If you are familiar with paradoxical intervention or the reverse paradox induction, you know that this method will induce trance. As they pretend they are hypnotized, they will wonder if they really are. This will produce genuine hypnosis through what is sometimes called the "as-if technique."

To Help Clients who Struggle with Letting Go

Whether the reason is physical or mental, sometimes clients just have a hard time letting go. Direct suggestion is great for this scenario:

I can sense you are holding on to some tension or even thoughts with your conscious mind.

Take in a deep breath, and as you exhale release all of that tension with your breath, letting go absolutely... all the way in, and all the way out. Excellent.

To Give Clients a Self-Directed Exit

The anxious client or client who really feels a need for control or safety will benefit from this suggestion when given early in the induction process:

> *As you experience this process of hypnosis, if at any time you are uncomfortable or nervous, or even just want to reorient to the room, it will be easy to do.*
>
> *No matter what I am saying or doing, at any time you will be able to count to yourself 1-2-3 and open your eyes feeling refreshed and alert.*
>
> *Anytime you need to do this, it is okay, counting from 1 to 3 in your own mind, and opening the eyes.*
>
> *I will then stop and let you express yourself, and we can talk about any concerns you might have....*

When Clients Swallow, Scratch, Itch, or Fidget During a Session

Clients will scratch, itch, move, swallow, and fidget. Much of this is unconscious, and clients often are unaware that they are doing this during a session.

If you have someone who really moves, itches, and fidgets, excessively during a session, when you have finished, ask them if they were aware of it, and if it bothered them. Ninety-nine percent of the time they were unaware of these actions. Usually it is more troubling to the hypnotist than the client.

But when clients begins itching, moving, swallowing, etcetera, I usually say this:

> *It is perfectly okay to scratch an itch, adjust for comfort, or swallow at anytime during our session. In fact, it makes it even easier to further your hypnotic state.*

If a Client "Twitches" or has a Muscle Spasm

As people enter relaxation, involuntary muscle responses may result in twitching or spasm. Some of these can even startle the client or the therapist.

If the client continues with eyes closed as if nothing happened:

> *Many people as they enter sleep or trance find the muscles relax and twitch involuntarily. This is of course normal and is a sign you are doing well and can continue to relax...*

If client is startled (or embarrassed) and opens their eyes:

> *It's okay. Open your eyes! As one enters sleep or trance the muscles sometimes relax and twitch. I am sure you have had this happen in bed right before sleep.*
>
> *You can close your eyes again now, knowing this is normal and okay, even a good sign telling yourself you can easily go into deep trance.*

When Clients Sneeze During the Session

Clients will start to sneeze at the darndest times, usually right after the induction. Here is what to say when this happens:

Open your eyes. You sneezed, so I had you open your eyes so you could clear your sinuses.

Don't worry; it will be easy for us to begin again right where we left off. There is a box of tissues right next to you, and I'll give you minute if you need to use them.

In fact, clearing out the sinuses at any time during our session will help you to be more comfortable and will not stop your mind from being able to do the work.

So now close your eyes, and if you need to get another tissue at any time, just open your eyes, and get one.

To Deal with Tears During Trance

Here are some ideas for dealing with tears, both the expected and unexpected tears.

If they do not open the eyes and there is just a tear or two:

> *As you take this time for yourself, you may notice your eyes water or even notice a tear. This is a healing process, and you are where you need to be, doing exactly what you need to be doing, so you can embrace this experience and go deeper into hypnosis.*

If they do not open their eyes but let the tears flow:

> *Often in hypnosis, releasing tension also releases emotions, and these emotions are yours, represented by tears.*

> *I have some tissue on the table next to you, and you can open your eyes and use them at anytime, or you can embrace this natural process of healing and continue to go deeper into hypnosis.*

If they open their eyes, and appear embarrassed or unsure of what to do:

> *A lot of people have tears when they make change, sometimes for no identifiable reason other than they just do.*

> *Here is a box of Kleenex* (hand them the box), *and feel free to let your emotions flow.*
>
> *You are in a safe place and when you are ready, let me know, or just close your eyes and we will continue with the progress you have already made.*

If they open their eyes, and appear panicked, angry, or have other unexpected and intense emotions:

> *Take in a breath. Familiarize yourself with the room. Feel the floor below your feet.*
>
> *Everyone who comes here is allowed to have intense emotions* (hand them Kleenex).
>
> *You are here, safe in this office. It is today, and right now in this place you are here, in the present.*
>
> *We can continue in a minute, or we can even stop the session for now and take a moment to talk about what you need at this moment.*

To Deal with Intense Unpleasant Emotion

Occasionally, unexpected or unpleasant emotions come to the surface in hypnosis. Most people do not manifest this, but it happens, even when the suggestions I give are all positive, and I intentionally avoid producing abreaction.

However when it does occur, here are some scripts that are useful.

If their eyes remain closed and they appear to be in deep trance:

> *Pay attention now to the floor below you and the chair you are sitting in.*
>
> *You are here where you need to be, but open your eyes. Open your eyes for a moment.*
>
> (ask about comfort and wellbeing and return to trance if appropriate)

If eyes open and they exit trance:

> *Difficult emotions can be a key to moving forward. It is okay to have emotions, even intense emotions.*
>
> *When you are ready we can continue.*

To Change your Plan or Style to a New One

Every now and then I will go into a suggestion using one style, and then for some reason decide to shift and do something entirely different.

Here is what I say:

To this point I have spoken to you using techniques and language that many are familiar with. I am now going to shift my tone and change to (a more direct method, or any other method), and this will help you to more easily experience deep trance.

To Introduce a Written Script

A lot of hypnotists are self-conscious about reading from a script or book, believing the claim from other hypnotists that they never use a script.

My guess is that the people who make this claim are often ineffective or in reality do not do much hypnosis. If you see six to ten clients a day, using a script or an outline will help you stay focused and help you to be more effective.

Here is what I say to clients to prepare them for these readings:

As you relax, you may hear me reading from a book, or even from my notes.

The reason is simple: I want to make sure that I cover everything that is important to you, and so at times, I may read for you a passage from a book, or a story, or even read from my notes.

This will help me to make certain that I cover everything you came here for today, and by hearing these readings, you can be assured that this session of hypnosis is complete.

To Set Up a Story, Parable, or Metaphor

I like to read stories, parables and metaphors to clients. These can come from current books or even historical texts, like the Bible or Aesop's fables.

Here is what I tell clients about the stories I read:

As you relax, I am going to tell you a story. Although this story was not written specifically about you, I am certain your subconscious mind will recognize the truth in this story that is useful to you.

Your conscious mind might not be able to make sense without really thinking, but the subconscious mind is intuitive and will easily be able to learn from this story.

To Read from a Script

Like reading a story, parable, or metaphor, reading from a script can help you stay focused. Of course, scripts should be tailored to the individual client, and you should be prepared to deviate from any written script as the client's reactions dictate, but scripts help promote structure and help you to use multiple techniques without missing anything that is important.

To do this well, you should pre-read any script you didn't write (and even those you did). Practice reading it aloud, as many times as possible before the session, so that when the time comes you are familiar with the content and pacing, and can then read it flawlessly without error.

> *I want to make certain that I cover everything that is important to you, and so I have a script that I often use with people who are* (insert problem here).

> *This script is a guide for me; it helps me to remember everything that is important to you.*

> *So if it sounds as if I am reading, I will be, and I will be reading that which many others have found helpful.*

To Transition to Direct Suggestion

I usually start out my suggestive therapy with indirect suggestion, stories, and other indirect methods of learning. I then usually follow with a transitional deepener and move into direct suggestion. Here is what I say:

I am now going to give you direct suggestions.

These are suggestions that you immediately and without hesitation act upon.

These suggestions are called direct suggestion, because I will tell you what the outcomes of this session will be.

You know this to be true because you have already been able to create trance, and deep relaxation, and you can now create action that solves your problem.

To Deepen Trance

Deepeners and transitional deepeners are explored in more detail in one of my earlier books, *Inductions and Deepeners: Styles and Approaches for Effective Hypnosis*. But learning standard patter to help a person deepen trance is very useful.

With a formal deepening process, a few lines can take a client to the next level. These can be used transitionally at any point during a session, and I personally tend to use various deepeners throughout a session, multiple times.

> *Notice how easy it is to go into an even deeper trance. You can notice this by noting how your heart rate has become even more smooth and rhythmic, and by how good it feels to enjoy this time.*
>
> *And so double the sensation of relaxation, in both mind and body, going even deeper into trance, accessing that part of the mind where creativity is born, intuition exists and where deep trance feels most comfortable.*

Transitional deepening is useful. Throughout my sessions I am frequently 'deepening' trance with sayings like this:

> *Take in a deep breath... and exhale. Noticing your breathing has slowed, and your heart rate is smooth and rhythmic.*
>
> *Now let yourself fall into deep trance, by doubling the sensation of relaxation with each breath.*
>
> *Again inhale. Now exhale, breathing out any resistance to change, deeply relaxed.*

To Count to the Deepest Level of Trance

Hypnotists tend to obsess about trance depth. I usually want my clients to be deep enough to demonstrate basic phenomena, but I do not worry about trance depth for the most part. However, this patter is useful for bringing a client to very deep levels, and is especially useful in pain management or pre-surgical preparation.

> *Notice how both mind and body are relaxed, in fact so relaxed that although you know you could open your eyes if you wanted to, it feels so good to let them stay closed.*
>
> *So relaxed that your hands feel warm and heavy, so heavy you cannot move them, even though you know you could.*
>
> *Try to move your hands, and find they become heavier and heavier, feeling good, to just let them sit.*
>
> *And now, deep trance.*
>
> *Deeper and deeper, 5-4-3-2-1-0, no longer paying attention to each word but rather just experiencing this process. Letting all of your muscles relax. Down deeper, and deeper.*
>
> *Again, 5-4-3-2-1-0, accessing that part of the mind you are rarely conscious of, but that vast reservoir of learning and knowledge.*

When Clients won't Go into Deep Trance

Clients benefit from hypnosis whether in deep trance or light trance. In fact, most clients cycle up and down throughout a session between various levels of trance, which is normal and perfectly acceptable.

However, I have found this patter helps promotes deeper trance levels:

> *With your conscious mind you may be listening carefully to each word, or even paying attention to the sounds around you, to the music you hear or even to the air in the room.*
>
> *Many people have learned that deep trance, or trance where one no longer pays attention, is not necessary for true and lasting change.*

In fact, many have learned how to pay attention and go into deep trance at the same time - and so you can pay attention carefully with the conscious mind or let go now, noticing how good it feels to really enjoy this time of profound relaxation and learning.

To Create Hypnotic Experience

In my office, I use headphones and speak through a microphone to do hypnosis. This detaches the client and creates a "special" event for them, the experience of hypnosis.

I also do this through my words, ratifying the process they have undertaken to help them note the "specialness" of what they are accomplishing:

> *Notice how you have easily pushed the distractions of the day aside, easily creating your own special hypnotic experience.*
>
> *It's as if you are a million miles from any concerns, deeply relaxed and focused on exactly where you need to be right now at this moment.*

To Create Comfort

Clients come to us with emotional pain, physical pain, and stress. Here is a specific technique that can be used to increase comfort in any hypnosis session, or as a suggestion in pain management hypnosis:

You have already relaxed your body and relaxed your mind (in the induction), *and now it is time to create comfort.*

This comfort can be emotional, like security or significance, or even physical, and even in bones or muscles that have held pain or stress.

The easiest way to do this is by imagining an old time radio, the one with a volume knob that is turned. And imagine it is set on zero to start, but you can turn it to the right, number by number, all the way to ten.

And imagine that with each number, seeing yourself turning that knob to a level one, and two and three, your comfort increases.

Just as you were able to increase your relaxation earlier, you can increase your comfort (specify where or how) with each number, turning it to a four, five and six, continuing to increase your comfort, all the way to number ten...

To Help Clients Realize they are Going into Hypnosis

Using a "convincer" *during* a session is a powerful tool for ratifying hypnosis and promoting deep trance. Here is patter for moving the convincer from the pre-talk to the actual session, usually following the deepener:

Notice now that you feel differently at this moment than you did a few minutes ago or even when you walked in the door.

And notice how although you know you could open your eyes it feels so good to relax, then when you try to open them they become even more comfortable and they now become locked down tighter with deep relaxation. Try to open them—but find it impossible, locked down with heavy relaxation.

This is hypnosis, a state you have created, and a state of learning and creativity...

To Manifest Initial Hypnotic Phenomena

When clients feel or experience change as a result of the hypnotic process, they believe that change is possible. I think it is important in any induction to produce sensations, because it allows a person to think, "Wow, I'm being hypnotized!"

I borrow the following lines from the autogenic-awareness induction, and apply them regardless of what type of induction I actually use, producing the first phenomena during a session:

Now think of the word warmth, and think of the word heavy. Warm and Heavy.

Now focus on your hands resting on your lap, and say to yourself, "My hands are warm and heavy; my hands are warm and heavy."

Let yourself feel a sense of warmth in your hands and note the heaviness you feel in those hands.

Of course, you know you could move them if you wanted to, but they are so very heavy it is easier to just let them lie still as your whole body becomes comfortably warm and heavy.

To Facilitate Two-Way Communication

I want clients to communicate with me and talk to me during sessions. Too often the perception of hypnosis is that the client sleeps while the hypnotist talks. This is far from reality, and as you become more experienced you will communicate more and more often with clients in hypnosis.

As you go deeper into hypnosis, you will always be able to hear my voice.

In fact, you will always be able to talk to me, or communicate by answering my questions at any time.

And of course you will always be able to follow my instructions, no matter how deep you experience trance.

When I ask you questions, or share a thought, you will be able to remain relaxed and in hypnosis, but be able to answer me at anytime without being disturbed.

In fact, the sound of your own voice will simply relax you further.

To Keep Client Awake During Mid-Session

Although clients rarely sleep during a session, I use this to help me keep a client awake if I think they have slipped into delta levels of brain functioning.

Sometimes it is hard for me to tell if one is awake or deeply relaxed.

And so, open your eyes for a moment, remaining relaxed but opening your eyes.

(Client opens eyes)

Perfect. You have the ability to remain relaxed yet awake.

Closing the eyes now, becoming even more relaxed. Never asleep but deeply relaxed.

If client does not open eyes, pause, and say:

It feels good to relax, but now open your eyes.

I will count from one to three, and on the count of three open the eyes.

1-2-3 (snap).

Perfect. Now, close the eyes again, becoming even more relaxed. Never asleep but deeply relaxed.

To Decrease Resistance at Any Time in the Process

I find direct suggestion is best for reducing any resistance. Here is a good script for countering resistance and encouraging compliance:

Give up anything known or unknown keeping you from going deep into trance or from accomplishing _____.

Imagine a snowman created from late winter snows, and imagine as the springtime sun warms this creation, it melts, quickly and totally.

As easily as the daytime sun can melt a snowman, you too can let go of and melt away anything known or unknown keeping you from experiencing trance (or success, or whatever).

To Employ a Double Bind

Milton Erickson was famous for using "double binds." His words would sound like they included a choice, but no matter what the client chose, the outcome would still be the same.

For example, going into trance quickly or going into trance slowly accomplishes the same thing: going into trance.

Other double binds you can create are:

Give up cigarettes easily, or give up cigarettes with a struggle.

Let pain gradually slip away over time, or let pain instantly disappear.

In both cases the result is the same.

The stream said to the river, you go quickly and I slowly, but together we will reach the sea.

It does not matter if you go into trance quickly or slowly; by the end of this session you will have reached your goals.

In fact, you have already achieved them by coming here today.

To Validate Progress

People need to be validated. Validating progress during a session is a powerful tool for success:

Do you notice how it already feels different than when you first walked into the door?

This is because change has taken place already, in part by simply walking through the door, but also by your incredible work during this session.

To Give Client Ownership of Suggestions

Clients need to own the suggestions that are given during hypnosis. People will not change just because some stranger said to, but rather because they internalized these suggestions and made them their own. Here is how to do this:

I am now going to give you some direct suggestions.

They really are not suggestions at all though, but rather are things you have asked me to tell you.

And you have let me know this by simply coming here today to resolve this issue.

And so the suggestions I make are actually not from me, but are from you, and therefore you take action on them without question, and immediately, knowing that this is what you have asked me to speak to your subconscious mind.

To Compound Suggestions

Compounding is a technique that is very useful. In direct marketing I have learned that people respond the third mail out, and in parenting I have learned that it often takes telling a kid three times to clean their room before it actually gets done.

Effective hypnosis incorporates our human tendency to comply or learn through repetition. I usually give direct suggestions multiple times through a session.

A few moments ago I listed some direct suggestions, and as you relax I am going to give you these same suggestions again.

The reason is simple, repetition is a key to success, and so let yourself go into even deeper trance.

5-4-3-2-1-0.

As I help you learn through repetition, covering these same suggestions again.

To Avoid Sounding like a Psychic or a Fortune Cookie

New hypnotists giving direct suggestions often sound like a psychic or fortune teller, prognosticating the future. They say things like, "You will only eat healthy foods" and "You will no longer smoke."

The answer is to always tie any future action to present action. For example, if they are no longer going to eat all they can at the buffet, how would we know that? If we tie future action on the part of the client to present (or even past) action, the prognostication angle seems to disappear.

Try using language like this:

> *And when you find yourself at a buffet, with so many opportunities to make healthy food choices in the correct portion, you no longer eat all you can, instead acting on the commitment you have made today, and see the buffet as it truly is, the chance to make healthy food choices you enjoy in the correct portion.*

To Have Client Take Action in Hypnosis

Hypnosis can be and should be an interactive process, with clients taking both specific mental and physical actions (like demonstrating an anchor). Here is what I say to encourage specific action:

As you have learned by involving your mind in this process, hypnosis is not passive, like something that happens to you, but rather it is something that you create.

Creativity is the life of action, and now you are ready for the next step in your progress, moving from an idea and into action.

I am going to ask you to...

To Tap into Unconscious Resources

The subconscious mind is a vast reservoir of experiences, resources, and abilities. Some of these are known to the conscious mind, and many of them remain forever in the subconscious mind.

I use this patter near the end of my sessions:

And now let anything known to you or unknown to you that can be a source for power and success become a part of your action.

Let the resources and strengths you possess, even those you are as yet unaware of, be your guide and empower you to make change.

To Give Universal Reinforcers

Universal re-inforcers are a great tool for anchoring specific states to normal everyday experiences. They can even replace old responses to everyday experience.

For example, someone you are seeing for stress management can be reminded that when the phone rings (formerly stressful), they will be reminded of how good it feels to make change.

When I was a teenager, for whatever reason, our church leader always told us that when we saw a UPS truck it should be a reminder to us that Jesus loves us. Thirty decades later, I still think of Jesus when I see a UPS truck.

These universal re-inforcers can be positive lifelong associations. The anchor can be a color, an event, a sound, or anything that is a reoccurring pattern or experience in life.

Some hypnotists use the color red, giving the suggestion that whenever they see something red it will bring a positive response. Here is an example of the patter for setting a universal re-inforcer in smoking cessation:

> *And as one more suggestion, for some inexplicable reason, over the next day or two, over even three, whenever you see a delivery truck, you instantly and just for a moment, without going into hypnosis, be reminded of this place where you are today.*

You are reminded of how good it feels to make a commitment, to enter a new chapter of life and to be a non-smoker.

When you see a delivery truck, it brings a smile to your face, maybe even a chuckle, as you recognize you have been hypnotized and that you have the ability to succeed.

I chose a generic delivery truck as the anchor in this re-inforcer because a lot of smokers smoke in the car, and odds are good that every time they are in their car they will see some sort of delivery truck.

How to Give a Post-Hypnotic Suggestion

In reality, most suggestions are actually posthypnotic suggestions, but in the context of hypnotherapy we generally think of post-hypnotic suggestions as those given at the end of a session or even during the awakening phase.

I give the following suggestions (or an appropriate variation) to all of my clients, and so I have incorporated them into the awakening process.

> *It is now time to reorient to the room around you, and in a few moments I am going to ask you to open your eyes, feeling refreshed and wonderful.*
>
> *But before you open your eyes, recognize you have done great work today.*
>
> *And I am going to count from one to three, with each number you become more alert, more awake and more ready to open your eyes.*
>
> *One. Taking in a deep breath and feeling wonderful, recognizing it will be even easier to enter hypnosis in each and every future session.*
>
> *Two. Stretch out any muscles that need to be stretched, making time each day to listen to the CD I will be giving you,*
>
> *And three, wide awake, opening the eyes...*

Magic Words

How to Transition from Deep Trance to End of Session

A frustration for newer hypnotists is often figuring out how to move the client gracefully up from a state of deep trance and multiple suggestions to a state of being wide awake and alert. After all, no one wants to be roused from a good nap, and hypnosis can have the same effect.

Here is what I do:

And although we are nearing the end of our time, I am going to give you another minute or two to simply enjoy the tranquil peace you have created.

As you listen to the music in the background, continue to take another minute and feel good about the work you have done, even congratulating yourself, and then in a moment or so I will help you to feel energetic and be ready to take on the day....

To Make Sure the Client is Stable Following a Session

People talk about the "safety" aspects of hypnosis all the time, but rarely are they referring to falls. I am convinced that falls, in both clinical and other forms of hypnosis, are the number one area of liability.

For this reason, after every session, after their eyes are open and they are fully awake, I spend another moment making sure the client is stable.

Before you stand, take another breath.

Feels wonderful, doesn't it? Great.

Are you oriented?

Do you feel the floor below your shoes and feel stable? Perfect.

You can use the lever on the side of the recliner to make it easier to stand, just put it in the down position.

Awesome. You will do well.

To Schedule the Next Visit

I find scheduling a session immediately following the current session is the best way to make certain clients follow through and set the next session. I say this:

> *Before you go, let's look at the schedule and set our next meeting. I am free next _____ or _____ in the (mornings, afternoons). Does either of those times work for you, or is there a better time?*

To Leave the Room Mid-Session

Although it will not happen often, there are occasions the hypnotist might need to leave the room in the middle of a session. Perhaps it is something as simple as nature's call, or perhaps to respond to some outside crisis, delivery person or other unexpected interruption. One can, of course, emerge the client and have them reorient, then return to trance for essentially session two. Or, one can leave the client in trance, exit the room and return to complete the session. Here is how I have handled this:

> *As you relax deeper, 5-4-3-2-1-0 pay attention to your inner creative voice and the state of learning (or serenity) you have created. I am going to give you several minutes of alone time, to listen to your inner wisdom and draw from the strengths that exist within you to help you (insert problem to solve here).*
>
> *You may hear me step out for a moment, and then back into the room, but this is your time, your time tap into those resources within you that are most positive or to simply enjoy a few minutes of peaceful serenity.*

FINAL THOUGHTS

I hope you have found these suggestions useful. Again, they are just some of the ways I've learned over the years to positively answer client questions or questions I had about how to handle certain situations.

Some of them might even sound redundant, but that's okay—the point, again, is for you to get an idea of the language patter that is effective, and then customize it for both your own personal style and the individual client's specific needs.

If you ever have other questions, feel free to join the ICBCH discussion group at **www.ICBCHForum.com**, where I and dozens of other hypnotist interact almost daily on all things hypnotic.

Best wishes for your continued success!

APPENDIX A: SAMPLE INTAKE QUESTIONS

What do you want to accomplish with hypnosis today:
___ Stress Management
___ Quit Smoking
___ Weight Loss
___ Overcome Fears—Specify:
___ Test Taking
___ Medical Condition—Specify:
___ Pain Management
___ Sexual Difficulties
___ Other—Specify:

What is your prior experience with hypnosis:
___ None
___ Have been hypnotized at a stage show
___ Have been hypnotized one on one
___ Have listened to hypnosis tapes or CDs
___ Have read books on hypnosis
___ Have friends/family who have been hypnotized

What are your beliefs about hypnosis?
___ I think it can help me
___ I will try it and see what happens
___ I am a skeptic

What are your three biggest personal strengths?
1.)
2.)
3.)

HEALTH:
List all medical and mental health conditions for which you are currently being treated.

Magic Words

1.) Diagnosis:
Treating physician:
Medications:
(repeat this section 3-5 times on the form, for potential additional conditions)

List any other health concerns, fears, or issues:

List any other medications:

Do you drink alcohol?
___ Never
___ Once a month
___ Once a week
___ A few times a week
___ Daily

Do you smoke cigarettes?
___ Never have
___ Former smoker—If so, When did you quit:
___ Yes I am a light smoker—If so, How many cigarettes per day:
___ Yes I am a heavy smoker—If so, How many cigarettes per day:

Do you use marijuana?
___ No   ___ Yes—If so, How often:

Do you use other drugs?
___ Cocaine or other stimulants
___ Ecstasy or club drugs
___ Heroin or methadone
___ Unprescribed pain pills
___ Prescription pain pills
___ Prescription anti-anxiety medications (such as valium)
___ Unprescribed anti-anxiety medications
___ Other drugs—Specify:

Do you have sleep difficulties?
___ Rarely
___ I don't get enough sleep
___ I have trouble falling asleep
___ I have trouble staying asleep
___ I sleep too much

Eating Patterns:
___ I am on a special diet—Specify:
___ I eat mostly healthy foods
___ I don't eat regularly
___ I overeat
___ I do not eat enough
___ I binge eat
___ I purge myself when full
___ I snack too often

In my personal relationships, I am:
___ Unsatisfied
___ Sometimes satisfied
___ Mostly satisfied
___ I am very happy with my relationships with others

What do you do to handle tension and stress?

What do you do for fun?

What are your hobbies?

What do you want to accomplish with hypnosis?

Is there anything else you think the hypnotherapist should know?

APPENDIX B: ADDITIONAL ASSESSMENT TOOLS

Other useful assessment forms include the **"Nongard Assessment of Primary Representational Systems."** This one-page self-report helps you determine if the client is more visual, auditory, or kinesthetic, which can help you tailor your induction, suggestions, and patter to meet their personal primary processing or learning style. It is available free on my SubliminalScience.com webpage.

For clients seeking help with social skills, vocational advancements, and situational supports, the "**NSRI—Nongard Strengths and Resources Inventory**" is a great resource. The NSRI is a simple one-page assessment tool that can help quickly determine the client's own perception of their personal strengths, resources, and abilities. Having this information provides the hypnotherapist with clues to pre-existing attributes that can be useful to reinforce prescriptive scripts and track progress.

If you know that the client has some education, believes they work well with others, and has several healthy situational supports (friends, family, etc.), you can incorporate this information into the therapeutic suggestions, by reinforcing the importance of turning to these healthy relationships as a support system.

For example:

When you find yourself in a stressful situation, you know you can call your brother or one of your friends (name) for support, and just talk for a few minutes.

As for smoking assessments, there are a few good ones available that can really make a difference in your treatment approach. One is **The Fagerstrom Test for Nicotine Dependence: A Revision of the Fagerstrom Tolerance Questionnaire**, British Journal of Addiction, (1991)86, 1119-1127. This short quiz assesses when the client smokes, which can offer insight into their level of nicotine addiction. It also uncovers other key factors behind their dependency that will make it easier to create a cessation program that targets their specific needs.

Another great smoking cessation resource is the "**Nongard Nicotine Relapse Indicator Checklist."** We need to determine psychological, social, and physical indicators for potential relapse. Understanding what and how the client thinks about their tobacco use can help identify the potential triggers or 'red flags' that could cause stress or difficulty in the near or even far future.

It is important that the client continually feels encouraged by the positive changes they are making—for example, not using tobacco, eating nutritiously, exercising frequently, and so on. The faster they fall into these healthy habits, the better their odds of succeeding in the long-run. But a crisis can come—stressful situations may arise—and if they are not adequately prepared with healthy alternatives, they might give in and reach for that old comfortable habit of tobacco.

All of the assessment tools listed in this appendix may be located on the Internet.

INTERNET RESOURCES FOR HYPNOTISTS

www.ICBCHForum.com
This is a great free resource where Richard Nongard has posted scripts, teaching video, therapy forms and other resources for hypnotists. There is also a vibrant chat community here exchanging ideas.

www.Hypnothoughts.com
This is the internets largest free resource and social community for hypnotherapists.

www.SubliminalScience.com
This is the storefront for all of Richard Nongard's training DVD's, live schedule and other products

www.HypnotherpyBoard.org
This is the homepage of the fastest growing and most dynamic hypnosis professional association. Join the ICBCH today and become a member of this fast growing professional association.

Richard K. Nongard

Earn Certification as an NLP Practitioner and Life Coach

Enhance your skills and your credentials with Advanced Clinical Hypnotherapy Certification

www.SubliminalScience.com

Made in the USA
Monee, IL
07 August 2025